Tasting Rain

tasting rain

Bebe,

Enjoy the Rain!

Kim :)

KIM MALCHUK

forever books
WINNIPEG, CANADA
www.foreverbooks.ca

Tasting Rain
Copyright © 2010 Kim Malchuk

ISBN: 978-1-926718-06-4

Cover Design: Yvonne Parks Design
Book Design: Andrew Mackay
Managing Editor: Rick Johnson

Printed in Canada

Dedication

To the one who showed me life is filled with many beautiful colours and that it is not simply black and white, as I once thought. I want people to know that a "crazy kind of mutual love," as seen on the big screen or read about in books, really does exist. You just have to be ready for it and truly believe you deserve that kind of love.

To my "Bridges".
This was and is because of our love.
For Mel.

And

To all of my reasons, seasons,
and other lifetimes.
You know who you are
and I thank God for you every day.

Acknowledgements

In acknowledging the people who contributed to *Tasting Rain*, I need to begin with the institutions that gave me the greatest gifts of all—hope and time.

The National Cancer Institute in Bethesda, Maryland, provided us with the hope that we were searching for when told that there was none. Your institute was truly the silver lining in the very dark cloud that hovered over our lives when we were informed that cancer was going to be a part of our journey. I am forever grateful that we discovered your remarkable facility when searching for answers on the Internet. We were not going to settle in and just stand by and let this beast interfere with the magical life we were living. Should any readers find themselves in similar situations, I urge you to visit the website *www.cancer.gov* to learn more about the invaluable, life-saving services the institute can give those who are in desperate need and searching for another solution.

Thank you to the medical professionals at St. Boniface General Hospital in Winnipeg, Manitoba, Canada, for the gift of time, particularly Dr. Ralph Wong and Dr. Garnett Crawford for their consummate care, honesty, and professionalism. I not only wish to acknowledge how they performed their medical duties, but also to thank them for how they treated us as people and not a statistic or a disease.

Special thanks as well to all the staff in the Palliative Care Unit at St. Boniface whose compassion and care was never in short supply, and to the two earthly angels I had the privilege of getting to know and lean on for support, Kathy Kyryluk and Linda McKellar. You two remarkable ladies were always within arm's reach when I needed to lean on someone. Your dedication and the assistance you provided will never be forgotten and will always be treasured. To learn more about CancerCare Manitoba, visit their website at www.cancercare.mb.ca.

Two other extraordinary individuals deserve particular acknowledgement. Amanda LeRougetel first came into my life as a business associate but is now so much more. I turned to Amanda and asked her if she would do me the favour of editing my very rough manuscript. I am forever in debt to Amanda because she brought such intelligence and engagement to the editing of *Tasting Rain*. Her insightful questions and prodding helped me walk more deeply into the narrative of my story. I always welcomed her honesty and comments because I knew that Amanda wanted only what I wanted—to end up with a story that flowed well and kept the reader interested. Her expertise, high standard of quality and, most importantly, her friendship continue to make me be the best I can be.

Lori Mitchell, who, co-incidentally, also entered my life through a past business relationship, has become my biggest cheerleader and champion. Lori is a dynamic and highly energetic business woman who has achieved many professional successes over the years. Lori is the fiercely entrepreneurial President of Tomboy Tools Canada. To read more of her incredible success story, visit her website at www.tomboytools.ca.

Acknowledgements

I know that all of Lori's hard work and determination in the running of her business will pay off in leaps and bounds one day. I cannot wait to help Lori celebrate when that day arrives. I want to be there for her as she has always been there for me, especially during this whole process of getting *Tasting Rain* published. She is my mentor and her constant passion, humour, and encouragement for my success has left me speechless. To be able to talk to and bounce ideas off someone who has my undying respect, not only from a business perspective but also about life in general, has truly been a magical experience. With Lori in my corner, how could I be anything but successful?

I will not take credit for the precious gift that came from an unexpected source. People definitely come into our lives for a reason and I am so thankful that I met Lillian Zvanovec. In the very brief time that Lillian and I spent together we discussed the projects that we were each working on. When I mentioned that I had written a book, she asked me to explain the subject matter and what the title was. She was thrilled and excited listening to my story and at the possibility of what was in store for me with the future success of this unpublished piece of work.

Days after this first and only meeting, I received an email from Lillian, who apologized for perhaps putting her nose in where it might not belong but she just had to suggest something to me. She simply could not stop thinking about my story and the title I had chosen for it. Then it came to her. She said that it was a combination of the day's weather and the side bar conversation we had about life that led her to coming up with a much stronger title for my manuscript. When she suggested "Tasting Rain", I was dumbfounded but so unbelievably elated.

I think back to why the manuscript sat for almost two years before I pursued publishing. My story did not have the right name and was not ready to be released to the public. I send Lillian a million thank-yous for the naming of my "child".

Kim Malchuk

I was told by a wise woman (Amanda) that *Tasting Rain* would be published when the right publishers presented themselves to me. I am thankful and "forever" grateful that Gus Henne from Forever Books and I found each other. When my other champion, Lori, suggested that I contact Forever Books, the instant I went to their website www.foreverbooks.ca and read the opening line on their home page, I knew I had found the publisher for *Tasting Rain*. The line was "Helping Others Tell Their Story."

From the moment Gus and I started conversing, I knew I had found a home and a company that cared about *Tasting Rain* as much as I did. I thank and trust you, Gus, for your experience, expertise in the publishing and marketing business, and guidance in making my dream a reality.

I cannot neglect to thank the people who came into my life for a reason or a season. The roles they played in my journey have contributed to the person that I am today. The lessons and experiences I learned from these people were priceless. Out of respect for these individuals, their names have been altered to protect their privacy.

Finally, to my lifetimes, I wish to thank all of my family and friends who have always been so encouraging. The support and offering of help and assistance to get this project into readers' hands will never be taken for granted. I love and cherish you all.

KIM MALCHUK

Raindrops

Preface 13

Introduction 15

1. Awakening 17

2. I Would Like to Introduce You to 29

3. Welcome Home. 49

4. Something Has Changed. 65

5. A Warrior Among Us 79

6. A State of Numb. 97

7. Table for One 111

8. In Case of Emergency 129

9. Land of the Living. 139

10. My Season 149

11. Timing is Everything. 159

12. The Choice is Up to You. 173

Preface

We are living in a very exciting time. What makes this time so interesting is that we have discovered the incredible power within ourselves. It is because of this discovery that the momentum continues to grow and build us stronger every day. The ability for each and every one of us to change, evolve and decide what our reality will be is exhilarating. More and more people are convinced that the life of their dreams is really achievable. The good life is not only for the selected few or the elite, but for the world at large. The fruits of life are within our reach; all we have to do is go out on the limb to get it.

Tasting Rain is exactly about this strength we find within ourselves. There is no denying that life is bittersweet, just like rain. It sometimes gives us destructive storms that destroy and harm the life that we knew. But, it is within these storms that the universe is urging us to rebuild and create a new way of life. The beauty of rain is that it offers us new beginnings, each and every time it showers the gift of change upon us.

As we are becoming more in tune with our own powerful energy, or what many refer to as 'awakenings', they see their possibilities are endless. They have tapped into a state of aware-ness and can feel the magic that life presents to them every single day. When I talk to people who are living out their dreams, there is one common thing to which they all attribute their new found freedom. That common denominator is that they took action to make their dream become a reality. They would not sit still and shelve their dream, nor would they wait for others to roll up their sleeves to pitch in to help them achieve their goal. They, and they alone, were the driving force behind their creation. They became the master of their destiny.

This is where the vast majority of us fail in making our dreams become our everyday life. Dreams will remain dreams if we don't take the necessary action to make them come to fruition. It is as simple as that. My dream is to help others and this was the sole purpose of writing *Tasting Rain*. I am sharing with you, the reader, a portion of my life that will illustrate that by simply changing your thoughts, believing in yourself, you can achieve whatever it is you desire out of life.

I invite you to read my story and see the proof that we can overcome anything that the storms in life present to us. In the end, my hope is that you too, will want to taste the rain like we once did as young, innocent, and, hopeful children. Back to a time in our lives when we believed, beyond a shadow of a doubt, that dreams really do come true.

Enjoy the Rain!
Kim
September, 2009

Introduction

Why did I sit down so many months ago and think my story was one that needed to be shared with readers? Have I achieved something amazing, like splitting the atom or solving world hunger? Not yet, but give me time, because I have come to understand something pretty astounding. We are all capable of greatness. That is the bond that we, as citizens of this world, share. We are amazing creatures once we stop putting limitations on ourselves. We can achieve anything we want in this life if we truly believe in it. Now here's the funny thing. The "it" that I am referring to is—ourselves. If you believe in yourself, then the world had better be ready for you. If you honestly believe that you deserve and want what you say you want, then nothing can ever stand in the way of your achieving greatness—nothing at all.

I had been toying with the idea of writing a book for a long time and then one night, while lying in bed, I started my self-talk and said—"Why not?" I jumped out of bed and ran to the calendar, circled the date and wrote, "This is the day!"

The next night, I sat in front of my computer and the words just seemed to type themselves out. I kid you not. A few weeks and a few chapters later, I was shocked at what was transpiring before my eyes. My passion for the book only intensified as I dug deeper and deeper into my life lessons and I could see the possibility of what started out as a pipe dream turning into a reality—my reality.

The beauty of my story is that I am no different than you. I am just trying to get through one day at a time to find my way in this world in order to have the life I truly want and envision for myself. So you see, even though the circumstances of my life might be different from yours, we are the same in that we both have dreams and goals for our lives. It's because of this shared commonality I believe that my story can help answer some questions that you might be asking yourself at this stage in your life. Are you crazy to be asking yourself the really hard questions? Not at all! In fact, I would say it is probably the sanest and healthiest thing you could ever do for yourself, because it means you are opening yourself up to new possibilities and to a different kind of life. The life you are truly capable of living.

Chapter One

Awakening

What better place to start telling you my story than at the beginning.

I want to take you back in time to when I began to ask myself some pretty scary, but important, questions. Don't worry, it's not going to be one of those, "W*ell it all started in a small farm house in the coldest December since 1962. The seventh child of ...*" I would not do that to you. No, it was scarier.

I was thirty-seven years old and had been married for eleven years to a man who seemed to adore me; I had an established fifteen-year career and a beautiful house on the outskirts of the city. I had a life that most women would cut off their right arm for, except for one small thing—there was a stranger staring back at me from the mirror. I didn't know who that person was anymore and, what was worse, I didn't even know when the woman I knew had disappeared. I was completely lost to myself; the fun-loving, caring person I once was seemed to be missing in action, replaced with someone I did not like. This person was dishonest, unhappy, bitter, angry, tired, and, the most agonizing realization of all was that she was alone.

This person merely existed. She was not living life at all but just going through the motions of a so-called perfect life. This might sound a bit odd to you or maybe not. Maybe you have been in a relationship at one time in your life in which you felt empty. Maybe you felt yourself alone when you were supposed to be a couple. You found yourself doing things more often on your own as opposed to doing things together. Friends and family see the perfect couple and are envious of what they believe the two have shared and built over time. Meanwhile you are thinking to yourself, *"Oh God, if they only knew the truth!"* If you have ever been in a relationship like that, then you know exactly what I am talking about.

Why was I questioning the state of my marriage after eleven years? What was happening to me, and to the values of what marriage was all about that I had stuck to over these years? My view on marriage was that when two people married it was for life, no exceptions. There was no grey area, only black and white. How could I possibly be alone in a marriage? What was wrong with me anyway?

I remember I had tried to talk about my concerns with my husband, Mark, when these feelings kept nagging at me. We had been married for about eight or nine years at the time when I told him that I felt things were not right between us and had not been for a long time. I told him I had been feeling this way for many years and was hoping that things could change between us, but instead they only seemed to be getting worse. I was worried about this and suggested that perhaps I should see a professional about it, about me in particular. I was trying to take responsibility for the state of our marriage, because I knew the problem was with me and that I was terribly unhappy. I was the one always pulling back. I was the one who did not want to be intimate. I was the one who would rather stay at work than be at home. Sex to me had become just another chore that had to be done around the house and something that I no longer looked forward to.

Mark talked me out of seeing a therapist, saying that what we were going through was normal for a couple who had been together for years. He convinced me that because my job was so stressful things would get better eventually, when work slowed down. If things were still distant between us and not getting any better over time, then perhaps I should consider leaving my job to reduce the stress level to alleviate the pressure I was feeling. If I chose to do that, when and if that time came, he would stand behind that decision and we would get through it as a couple. It made sense to me at the time, but in my heart I knew I was no longer in love with my husband.

So why did I not say anything at the time that I had finally mustered up the courage to at least confront Mark about my unhappiness? It was because I hate confrontation. It scares me because of the memories of seeing how it played out when my parents attempted, ever so poorly, to try this act with one another. Let's just say it always ended badly with someone leaving the house, usually my father.

So because of this childhood fear, I was too scared to say it directly to his face, for fear of hurting someone who did not deserve to be hurt and because of the old memories that clouded my mind. But by doing that, I was not being true to myself and, in turn, was not being truthful with Mark. To make peace and not rock the boat, I remember convincing myself that I had done my bit by at least trying to talk about it. Yet secretly, I was hoping that by opening the floor to having the conversation, Mark would have said something along the line that he too was no longer happy with our partnership. But that was not the case and I should have known better. Mark never talked about feelings, wants or desires and maybe that was part of the problem. He just went with the flow of life and never expected anything more than what was presented to him or to us. He always did whatever I wanted to do and never told me what he wished or hoped for. This was when the "nice guy" routine grew a little too much for me to bear at times.

Life had become boring and lonely because it was me who made all the decisions about the direction of our lives. It was a one-sided relationship, if you could even call it a relationship at all, and I truly missed having a partner who needed me. It's important to feel that you are needed and that was something desperately lacking in our marriage right from the start. We had, for so long, been living independently from one another and not doing much of anything as a couple, as a married couple should.

So what did we do after that conversation? We brought out the broom and swept the really big issues under the rug and hoped they would all go away. But they didn't, and the rift between us only widened over time.

Mark and I were married in 1988 when we were both twenty-six years old. You would think we were old enough to know exactly what we wanted out of a life and in a partner to share in that life. But I would not figure that out until many years later.

Before Mark came into my life, I had been working at developing my career for approximately three years. I was dating off and on within that time frame, more off than on, and nothing terribly serious. I was so driven back then to prove to everyone, especially to myself, that I was smart, worthy, and good enough to have it all. I would succeed in life despite what my mother had said I would amount to, which was not much of anything. I put everything on the back burner, relationships included, to prove I mattered. I was more interested in moving up the corporate ladder in the company that I was working for at the time. My goal was to leave my mark on this company, to become very successful, to be one of the youngest female executives the printing industry had ever seen. I was so focused on that goal that I lost touch with what really makes someone whole.

One day I came home after work to find a rose sitting at my door with a mysterious note inviting me out for dinner later that same week. Who could this be from? My social life was non-existent at the time. With a little detective work on my part, I was pleasantly surprised to discover that my secret admirer was Mark who, at the time, was living out of town. We had dated when we were both eighteen years old for a short time and then went our separate ways. Seven years later, he was back. We were able to pick up right where we had left off all those years before.

Things were always easy for Mark and me, effortless you might say. We dated for ten months and got married in the fall of 1988. Mark was a great catch: he was very good looking, athletic, funny, smart, a hard worker, incredibly organized, an all-round nice guy. Everyone was thrilled for us, but little did I know when I married him that the "nice guy" would eventually be the thing that would drive us apart. Our relationship quickly became one comprised of being best friends rather than husband and wife, but at the time, I didn't know any better.

Things for Mark and me could have been worse, right? We went through the years as status quo, friends, who both decided that careers were more important than bringing children into the mix. We shared a common goal and at least we were on the same page about that. Let's work ourselves to the bone to make up for all the toys and "stuff" we both did not have growing up. This is the way our marriage was for many years. We didn't realize it, but success came at a very high price. It was one of the big factors that cost us our marriage.

Today, when I hear people say they have married their best friend I want to warn them to be careful not to end up where Mark and I did. It is one thing to say that, but if you really end up treating each other like you would a best friend, perhaps that's the way the relationship should have stayed and you should not have jumped into a marriage so quickly. I would learn this important lesson about how to behave and treat a life partner, as a true equal, but not until later in my life's journey.

It was a couple of years after having that conversation with Mark about the problems with our marriage that I found myself feeling trapped in our "very quiet" arrangement. What do you do when you are the only one in a couple who feels the relationship is unhealthy? How do you go about telling someone who is a good person and would do anything for you that you are no longer "in love" with him? How do you tell him that because he is always so damn happy and that everything with him is just wonderful or that he doesn't need anything from you—that he is slowly driving you crazy? The questions and self-talk circling in my head did not seem to let up. If anything, they were becoming all consuming.

Then I asked myself the really big questions: How much longer will I be able to keep up this charade? Is it normal not to have passion in your marriage or in your life? Is it normal to never have an argument with your spouse because everything is just great and nothing is ever wrong? Is this all there is to life? It can't be. What? We are born, we are children, we go to school, we get a job, we get married (maybe have kids) and then we die? If that's it, then God has a great sense of humour and I can't wait to meet this comedian.

During this time, I can tell you that home did not feel like home. There was silence under that roof. No communication whatsoever. If Mark was not out in a sporting activity or staying late at work, I was out of the house, either at work putting in longer hours than necessary, or playing baseball in the summer evenings to avoid the dull existence of home life, and to avoid confrontation. So we filled our empty marriage with details instead of dealing with issues because that would have required energy and effort.

When you're depressed, like I was during those years, your energy level is very low, so it's easier to avoid issues than to address them head on. I simply did not want or have the energy to deal with what was becoming the inevitable fate of our marriage.

What was sadder was that it seemed to be only my problem. Mark seemed to be content with the status quo because if he was not, then why was he not saying anything to me about this strange arrangement? When we were home, Mark would be upstairs in the office working on the computer and watching some game on TV, and I would be in the basement watching a movie or losing myself in yet another novel. Just anything to escape from the loneliness that was hanging over me. I remember my genre of choice was legal/suspense/thrillers—no way would I even attempt to read romance novels. But every once in a while an author would throw in a steamy love scene and I would scoff at it, thinking, *"Yeah right, only in fiction or in the imagination of the writer, but not in real life—at least not in my life."*

I was so bitter and depressed with almost everything else in my life. The only thing that held any interest for me was playing baseball in the summer months. Pretty sad, wouldn't you say?

But I felt alive and happy when I was on my own or hanging out with the "girls". You learn to grasp onto the little things in life that make you happy so you can get through another day, week, month, and year. For me, it was summers. I was also secretly hoping to see someone, a stranger, who seemed to have captured my interest many years earlier. This stranger, in all likelihood, never even knew I existed and that was fine with me. It was safe for me and my troubled marriage.

I started losing weight during that time because I was stressing out about so many things. My life was falling apart, yet I was the only one who knew it. I was too proud, ashamed, and scared to let my secret out to anyone, for fear they would say I was crazy. My marriage was failing. I hated who I had become. I despised my job. My friends at the time were few and far between. I was so depressed I couldn't even stand my own company, so why would I subject my family and friends to me and my negative views on life? It felt like I was slowly choking to death on life—my life.

What was I missing? What was keeping me from the life I wanted and knew I deserved? I wasn't a bad person for wanting more out of life, so why was I feeling so damn guilty about it? With the new millennium approaching, could I go through another decade like this? There was one thing in my life I knew was desperately lacking and I was so thirsty for it. But what was it? Then, it hit me like a ton of bricks!

The "it" I was searching for was faith, although not the religious kind of faith. I did not run off to join a convent or some religious cult. Faith was right there in front of me the entire time, but I was too busy being skeptical and playing the victim to even see it. All I had to do was open my eyes and look around me. If I wasn't happy with my life, then I had to do something about it. I could no longer point the finger elsewhere. The problems in my life were ones I had created all on my own and I had to have faith in myself to turn my life around, stop pointing the finger and take responsibility for my choices.

It was as if I was looking at life through my own eyes for the very first time when this realization came to me. I was seeing and understanding certain things I had not seen before. I was asking myself these new and harder questions about the path that I was on and that was okay. It was more than okay. These questions were life-giving. I was looking at myself as an outside observer. Did I like what I was seeing? Did I even know who I was? Did I like myself or, more importantly, did I love the person I had evolved into?

The answer to all those questions was an astounding "No"! So then I said to myself, *"What are you going to do about it? Are you going to continue to play the martyr, the victim, or are you going to start making different choices for yourself?"*

I was terrified, but also excited, with my discovery. I felt as though I had just uncovered a great treasure. The precious gems I discovered were that I was in control of my own future and that I had to stop feeling guilty for wanting to experience more from life. I am in complete control of creating the life I wish to have, but I knew, in order to find myself, I would have to make some pretty bold changes. Changes that I knew in my heart I should have made long ago. I knew that my new choices were not going to be popular.

Was I ready to stand and face the world alone at thirty-seven? Did I have faith in myself to do this? What in the world was I basing my choices on, and why now? Was I ready to completely turn my comfortable, safe, and empty life upside down to finally satisfy that thirst? I was so scared to leave to start a new life of uncertainties, but even more frightened of what would happen to me if I stayed to live a life of certainties. I felt if I did not make a change, I would lose myself, my courage, and my way, forever. I could no longer continue to live this façade and deceive myself and Mark. It was too hard to stay and even harder to seriously think about leaving, but it was something I knew I had to do for myself. I had to be able to look into that mirror again and like who was reflected back at me.

I based my choices on the faith that I was doing the right thing for me and only me. Sometimes we have to be selfish in order to grow and that is not such a terrible thing to discover. I had stayed far too long, because I didn't want to hurt Mark or upset our friends and families. But continuing to live a life based on lies was no longer the answer for either one of us, especially for me. I needed to be true to my feelings. I was getting ready to leave a marriage that had died a long time ago.

I learned over the years not to cast blame on Mark, or me, for how our marriage had dissolved right before our eyes. We do the best we can with what we know and have at our disposal at the time. But don't kid yourself, I did question my sanity for quite awhile and quickly got myself into therapy before considering divorce as the final option. I needed help from an outsider, a neutral person who was not close to the situation, one who could be objective, who was trained in helping people who found themselves in trouble. I felt that I owed it to our marriage to at least try to salvage what we had built over the previous eleven years. Yet deep down in my heart, I knew that it was over for me. In the end, no amount of counseling was going to repair the damage, but I had to at least make an attempt.

I don't have many regrets in life, but the one that I did carry around for quite some time was that I hadn't listened to my inner voice when I first mentioned counseling to Mark as an option for myself. Would it have helped? I don't know, but I don't beat myself up over that decision any longer. I learned a valuable lesson because of that mistake. Listen to your inner voice and don't have others, even those who say they love you, convince you to go the other way. Have faith in what that voice is saying to you. It rarely leads you down the wrong path. I believe that counselors and therapists can be impartial parties for those who need to talk when they are faced with a crisis. We don't always have the answers ourselves, so it's okay to seek advice from those who are trained to help those in need. I was raised to believe that "shrinks", as they were often referred to, were simply a waste of money, that you don't air your dirty laundry in public, and the number one reason for not seeing a therapist was that if people ever found out, they would think you were crazy.

It was during this difficult time that I started questioning my belief system about a lot of things. I didn't think I was crazy to see a therapist. If anything, I believed the opposite and I started thinking differently about other things too. Maybe my idea about being married to one person for the rest of my life might be wrong as well? Do we only have one soul mate in our lifetime? Are we meant to be with only one person for our entire lives? I didn't know because this was the first time I ever questioned myself about that, and thought maybe not. Maybe some people are not fortunate enough to find and marry their ideal mate the first time around. Perhaps people stay in unhappy marriages because they fear being alone, or they stay for the sake of their children. If what society was saying about therapy was wrong, then there was a good possibility that the theory of "until death do you part" might be wrong as well.

Another fear that I knew would be realized was that family and friends, on both sides, would not side with me. My final decision to leave everything behind that I called my life up to that point was not going to be viewed favourably. I was going to be the bad guy and have to learn to live with that reputation for the rest of my life. Yet, knowing all the negative fallout from my choices that I was about to make, the relationships that would be severed immediately, and the unknown that stretched ahead of me, this was still something I was not going to let pass me by. What did I care about what others thought of me and my decisions? They were not living my life and it was about time I started to live my life the way I wanted to—not how others and society say I should live it. That's how I had been living my life up to that point and look where it got me. No, I needed to start listening to myself, to my inner voice, to have faith that the choices would be the right ones for me.

I would have to re-think my views on the values that I had developed throughout my life on certain issues. Maybe things in life are not always so clear-cut, black and white, or right or wrong. Maybe life is what *you* decide it should be, based on your own experiences instead of on your old ideals or how others say you should live it.

The reason I was doing this was to survive. I was trying to find out who I was. I was doing what was right for me. I felt there was a greater purpose for me and that this was not what life was all about. I was willing to leave everything behind to start anew in hopes of finding out what that purpose might be. Was I going to be making more mistakes by choosing to leave my marriage to be on my own, shelve a career that was changing how I viewed people in general, and alienating some friends and family to search for my purpose in life? I didn't think so; all I knew was that I was definitely willing to take the risk.

If you are taking risks you are living a life. I was so ready to embark on this new path that I literally left running and dared not look back for fear I might choose the easy way out and just stay, settle for an empty life and continue to play the victim. Something inside me was telling me that this was the right choice and the right time. It was okay to be asking myself these questions. My choices were based on faith in myself and nothing else. My life was about to take a different route, a different path, and I was excited for the first time in a long time. I was so looking forward to my new adventure, to the new mysteries that life was going to present to me. I was no longer asleep in my life. I decided to no longer play the victim and to start taking charge of my life. I was not helpless and this situation was far from hopeless.

What was even more thrilling was that I was finally going to meet and be introduced to the person whom I had been searching for all this time—my real self. I trusted and believed that the choices I was about to make were going to lead me right to her. I prayed that when I found her, I would love and be proud of her, no matter what. We were in this thing called "life" together and, once my decision to leave came to fruition, there was no turning back for either of us.

Chapter Two

I would like to introduce you to . . .

Mel. What kind of friend would I be if I didn't introduce you to the man who helped me find myself and still, to this day, is teaching me about life's mysteries? There would be no story about me if I didn't tell you about our story—the story from which my biggest life lessons have come.

I had first seen Mel in 1989 at a slo-pitch baseball game. Now remember, Mark and I had only been married a few months at that time. Mark's cousin convinced us to play baseball with her team that year and we thought it might be a fun, couple thing to do together.

Growing up, I was on a baseball team for only one season, when I was maybe ten or eleven, and that was it for my baseball experience. Luckily, I am a natural when it comes to certain sports and didn't completely embarrass myself when attempting to play this sport for what was really the first time in my life at the age of twenty-seven.

(Okay, getting back to the first time I laid my eyes on Mel.)

It was a beautiful summer evening and both teams were warming up, getting ready to play a double-header. I don't know why, but I took a special interest in watching this particular person drive up on his motorcycle. I had never been interested in motorcycles, or who drove them for that matter, until I saw this man get off his bike and take off his helmet. I was standing there just staring and thinking to myself that he must be here for a Marlboro Man photo shoot.

(For readers unfamiliar with the national advertising campaign set back in the late 70s and 80s, I will try to give you a visual. The Marlboro cigarette ads always featured a cowboy/rancher in faded Levis sitting on a horse with a Marlboro in hand, usually set in the Rockies. The models were always handsome, outdoorsy, sexy, and resembled the likes of Tom Selleck.)

Oh my! What a beautiful creature. He exuded this manly, rugged, masculine, "I can protect you from any kind of danger" aura. The only thing missing was a cowboy hat, cigarette, and a horse. *(Okay, so do you think he caught my attention?)*

I remember thinking at that moment how sad it was that I had never felt that kind of exhilaration for my own husband and wondered if that was normal between a husband and wife. I was getting a sign early on in my marriage that things may not be right with my level of attraction to my own husband. It made me nervous to even think that maybe I had made a bad decision in marrying Mark. Did I get married for the right reasons? Did I rush into it too quickly? It was something I did not want to start questioning myself on because I was scared of what the answers might be. I decided to take the easy way out and become an ostrich. Just stick my head in the sand and not look at what was staring me right in the face. I was going to avoid the tough questions and just live with my decision no matter how great the cost. I was NOT going to be a failure in this marriage and definitely NOT going to be the cause of the breakup of our union. The word "divorce" was not even in my vocabulary. I was NOT going to admit to the world that I might have made the biggest mistake of my life because, to me, the institution of marriage was sacred.

Remember what I said earlier. Growing up, my belief system was that when two people entered into marriage they did it once and it was for a lifetime, no questions asked. So I stopped asking myself questions. I decided not to listen to that pesky little voice inside my head and not pay any attention whatsoever to how this stranger made me feel. *It will pass,* I said to myself. I didn't know at the time but that tiny, little voice that popped up in my head when I least expected it was my inner voice, my greater self, trying to make me stand up and take notice. I would one day finally listen to that voice and try not to second guess what it was trying to tell me.

(Okay, so I'm a little stubborn and set in my ways; it took me eleven years to really listen.)

As it turned out, Mel wasn't there for a photo shoot after all. No, he was going to be our umpire for the evening and I recall thinking to myself, *"Please God, don't have them put me in as back catcher tonight."* If you are unfamiliar with the game of baseball, the back catcher crouches down behind home plate to catch the pitched ball and the umpire stands directly behind the catcher—just mere inches away from each other. Well, do I even have to tell you what position I ended up playing that evening? Yeah, you guessed it, and if that wasn't enough, I played so well in that position in game one, my reward was to play there for the second game of the evening as well. Oh lucky, tortured me. I remember that I could smell his cologne and it drove me completely crazy.

(Okay. I am going to have a little sidebar with you at this point in the story because, moving on, I will be using a term that I want you to understand. I think we all do it. We all define or view things in our own way based on past experiences, memories, or just gut feelings about things in general. So when I am about to give you my definition of life situations, I will refer to

*them as Kim + definition = "Kiminition". My analogies through-
out this book are not based on research studies or actual docu-
mented facts. They are my life experiences, which I wish to share
with you.)*

Here comes my first Kiminition: how I dealt with this awkward discovery:

*I convinced myself that having this exciting and titillating
feeling about a complete stranger was totally healthy. I should
not worry about not feeling that way about my own husband.
Just file that image of this stranger in my memory bank, never
do anything to act upon those lustful feelings, and everything
will be alright. Your partner is the person who you said you
would be with for all of eternity. Your spouse is loyal, steadfast,
accommodating and then ... you live happily ever after!*

Do you believe it? I convinced myself that having an average
level of attraction for my own husband was completely acceptable, especially when everything else was so good. But I was
thinking this after being married for not even a year. *Oh boy, I
was in trouble and I didn't even see it coming: or did I?* I got
scared, so I just ignored it and started the self-talk again to convince myself that things were okay. I mean, something's got to
give, right? It can't all be perfect and maybe, just maybe, it will
get better over time.

Mark and I were not abusive to one another. We lived in a
nice house. We were great friends. Our marriage was a complete
success, minus the sexual part of it. Over the years I continued to
convince myself that this was the price I had to pay for having a
fairly decent marriage. So, then, why was I letting my mind wan-
der so much? Why was I having fantasies about Mel, when I
barely knew him? Why did I continue to have them sporadically
for years to come? Why was I questioning the terms of my marriage—the terms that I had written and agreed to? Why did I
look at my partner more as a friend or brother than a husband?
I convinced myself that this behaviour was normal—not for just

a few weeks or months. No, I let myself believe it for almost my entire marriage.

It was the 90s—the era of the yuppies. Everyone was working crazy hours, having absolutely no work/life balance, filling their lives with events and details, and most couples were complaining about the lack of sex in their marriage anyway. Because everyone else was living like this, I believed what I was feeling was acceptable, the norm, how married life was. I would have to stop examining my marriage and just move on.

So over the years, to compensate for the emptiness in the partnership, Mark and I bought all the latest and greatest toys to show off to all our neighbours, family, and friends that we'd made it as a couple—we had it all. I mean, if we were working ourselves to the bone and sacrificing our relationship in order to have all the "stuff", well let's at least have something to show for the sacrifice. We don't have any children, so let's get a big screen TV. There! This will show everyone that we are really happy and a successful couple.

I realized I was comparing my marriage to what I knew growing up, to my role models—my parents. There were never any screaming, fighting, or drunken rages with Mark and me so, in my mind, my marriage was fantastic compared to my childhood example. I had achieved better than my parents, except that Mark and I had become roommates rather than husband and wife.

My parents did not have it all, not even close, but the one thing they did have was passion. Perhaps it was misguided, but it was there nonetheless. My God, they had seven children so it couldn't have been all that bad. Okay it was, but you know what I mean? A marriage without passion is dead in the water and if you don't do anything to save it, it's going to go under.

If I had only known then what I know now, my life would have turned out completely different. Would I have started more arguments to create passion between Mark and me? Would I have gotten into a drunken stupor to get me some action and to numb myself? Would I have changed any of my past experiences for that matter, if I had had the chance? No, because I believe that all of us are continually learning lessons throughout our journey in this lifetime. We have to figure things out on our own when the experience presents itself to us and examine our preconceived ideas about what is right and wrong.

What is right or wrong for one person may not be for another. I'm convinced that the hardest, yet most significant lessons to learn usually come from the most difficult challenges we face in our lives. It was only when I was making the decision to separate from Mark that I was able to start forgiving myself for the mistakes I had made in our marriage.

While on this journey, we are going to make mistakes because that is what life is. There is no How-To book in our public libraries that I am aware of, perhaps called, "Living Life Without Mistakes for Dummies." It would be nice, but it's just not that simple. We have to figure life out as we walk and stumble along the path.

When I realized that it was okay to finally admit that I had made mistakes and did not have to have all the answers, I was able to start forgiving myself. I was getting stronger and trusted the faith I had in myself that separation was the only option for me near the end of our marriage. I knew that to move forward and grow, I needed to forgive myself for my past mistakes and stop beating myself up over them. I had to stop feeling guilty that I fell out of love with my husband. If I could not learn to forgive myself, how could I possibly learn to forgive others for the mistakes they have made along their journey? Mahatma Gandhi said, *"The weak can never forgive. Forgiveness is the attribute of the strong."*

To forgive someone does not mean that you agree or condone what has happened. It just means that it's over and done with and, hopefully, they too, have learned something from the experience—good or bad. Nobody can change what transpired in that experience. It's in the past so, to move forward, you have to let it go. This is something I try to remember every day when going through the mystery of life. We do the best we can at the time, with the tools and self-knowledge we have at that point. If you don't know any better, how can you do any better? You can't. So learn to forgive yourself. It makes your life so much lighter, easier, and it makes you stronger in the end. It lightens the daily load that you carry around with you wherever you go.

We are not our yesterdays; we are not our pasts. We have the chance to change and renew ourselves every day, if we choose to. It is our decision to make. This is another lesson I have learned over the past few years. God, or whoever you believe in, has given us free will to do whatever we want to do with absolutely no judgment and that is a fact. When we make a bad choice about something, no lightning bolt shoots out from the heavens to strike us down and tell us that we have just screwed up.

The same can be said when we make a good choice. We don't see an army of angels singing our praises when that happens. Why? Because we are given free will to do whatever it is we choose to do. Learn and grow from those choices, but also realize that with the choices we make come consequences. We are who we are today because of the choices we have made every day of our waking lives. It took me awhile to figure that out and learn to accept it.

We all want to take responsibility for all the good that happens in our lives because it's easy, it's fun and it's self-gratifying. But the bad things that happen to us? Well, let's just say it's kind of funny how we don't want to take responsibility for those choices. A bad choice is like a bad rash. We just want to get it off our bodies as quickly as we can and disassociate ourselves from it.

People do not want to accept the responsibility for all the drama they invite into their lives, because it means they have to evaluate themselves, their thoughts, their beliefs and morals and, frankly, that's too difficult. It takes too much energy. It is so much easier to point the finger someplace else, continue to play the victim and say it's everyone else but not me.

Well, that was me, the victim. I was blaming everything and everyone, including Mark, for the problems occurring in my life instead of looking at what I was doing myself to bring it on. I knew that I had to make different choices if things were going to change in my life and I had to take responsibility for those choices. I was getting stronger because I was able to forgive myself and accept the role I played in the marriage. I was tired of being the victim and wanted to play a different role in my life.

It was now the winter of 1998, right around the time when I was considering a trial separation after all the self-talk and questions I had been asking myself for so long. One particular night, a good friend of mine, Dave, who also happened to play hockey with Mark, called the house to speak with Mark about their upcoming game. Dave and I had been friends since we were in junior high school and he is like a "brother from another mother". I just adore this man because we share something in common—our off-the-wall sense of humour. When we are together, we try to see who can make the other laugh until we almost wet ourselves.

I had reconnected with Dave at a baseball diamond, of all places, after not seeing this dear friend for many years. It was not only a huge and pleasant surprise to see that he had become an umpire in the same league I had been a part of for over ten years, but also a shock to see who he had chosen to become fast and furious friends with. Yes—you guessed it, my childhood friend had become great friends with my secret fantasy partner. *(Great! God does work his miracles in mysterious ways—does he not?)*

By this time, because of the separate lives we were living, Mark had stopped playing ball. I continued to play in a women's league during the summer months, because I had grown to love the sport. I did not want to see this activity come to an end just because Mark was no longer interested in it. It became my escape and something that made me feel alive.

Before I called Mark to the phone, Dave asked me very innocently if I knew who Mel was. His question threw me into a tailspin. Why would he ask me this out of the blue? I almost wanted to confess to my dear friend right at that moment my deep, dark secret about Mel. How I thought about him ever so briefly over the years. How, for some reason, this stranger captured my attention and interest from afar. Out of fear and confusion about the state of my marriage I decided this would not be the appropriate time to divulge this tidbit of information. So I did what I had become accustomed to during those years. I lied and pretended that everything was fine and simply did not want to talk about the doubts that lingered in my life. It was easier to hide those feelings than to confront them head on.

When I said yes, I knew who Mel was, my thoughts quickly shifted gears yet again. I wondered if Mel could have asked Dave about me, because Mel knew that Dave and I were such good friends. Did Mel want to know what my personal situation was because he was attracted to me? Was I available? Would I be interested in an older, experienced man?

I quickly snapped out of it, left the mini-conversation I was having all by myself in my head and rejoined reality to listen to what Dave really had to tell me. When it finally registered what Dave was saying, it was as if his foot had come through the phone line and kicked me right in the stomach. He told me that Mel had been diagnosed with kidney cancer and the prognosis was dismal. The cancer was terminal and they hadn't given him a lot of time. This man who was a picture of health, who had a beautiful physique, a healthy glow to his complexion and a laugh that was so hearty—had WHAT? There had to be a mistake. This could not be happening. I couldn't believe my reaction to this news. I had uttered maybe fifty words to Mel over the past ten years—mostly, "Hi. How are you?" But in my dreams, well, we knew each other intimately.

I finally handed the phone over to Mark and remember going downstairs and just sitting there, letting the terrible news sink in about Mel's health. My mind was racing with a million thoughts, and then I started thinking to myself, "*What in God's name are you thinking? Hello, earth to Kim. Get a grip on yourself. You're married. You have your own life, even though you can't stand it any longer and want to run away and join the circus. Don't you have enough problems of your own? You don't even know this man. This man doesn't even know you. Even if he did, don't you think he would have more important things on his mind right now, all things considered?*"

I could not believe that the health of this stranger could have such an effect on me. My thoughts quickly changed and went down a totally different avenue. It was the first time it had ever occurred to me over the years. Did this man have someone special in his life? Was there a wife, a girlfriend? Was there a woman sitting by his side at this moment, terrified at the thought of losing this man to cancer? My heart went out to her, whoever she was.

The '99 baseball season was underway for another year. I was happy that the summer had finally arrived, so I could get back to playing ball and having my escape for yet another season. Baseball was my saving grace at the time because it provided me with so many positive outlets. It got me away from a job that was sucking the life out of me. It gave me an opportunity to spend time with a bunch of great women and have a lot of laughs. It gave me my only source of exercise at the time, but, more importantly, it got me out of the house that I was so lonely in, even though my husband was right there.

It was during that summer that I was going to ask Mark for a trial separation, once I mustered up the courage to broach the subject again. Then, one weekend, I was playing in an out-of-town annual baseball tournament and was shocked when I saw Mel standing behind the plate, calling the game on one of the diamonds I happened to walk by.

The last time I had seen him was approximately two months prior to this tournament at one of our women's regular weekly games. He looked weak and terribly thin. The reality of his having cancer had finally sunk in. I had heard from Dave that Mel had already undergone an operation to remove his kidney and had been through a rigorous chemotherapy treatment, which had all taken place in Washington, DC.

When Mel was first diagnosed with cancer, the doctors said there was nothing they could do for him and that he should start getting his affairs in order. Mel was only forty-seven years old, with so much life still left to live. He was not going to accept that answer and he took his health into his own hands. Friends and family researched alternative treatments, clinics, and research/test groups on the Internet. All the searching had paid off. The National Cancer Institute in Bethesda, Maryland, was conducting studies. They were accepting candidates from anywhere in the world to be part of their clinical research and therapies. Mel, along with his acting physician at the time, jumped at the opportunity to participate in these studies. Mel felt that this might be his only hope for more time but totally understood going into the experimental study that there were no guarantees when cancer played a part in your life.

I knew that Mel had just returned home from Washington and was recuperating from his operation and chemotherapy treatment. I guess he had come out that evening to just sit back, enjoy the beautiful summer evening, and perhaps catch a game or two. I wanted to say something to him then, but decided against it. I had never spoken with him up to that point, so if I had started a conversation with him out of the blue, he probably would have wondered why. And really, did he want anyone to say anything to him? Maybe he was out for the evening just to get away from his own thoughts, just like I was, and not think about his situation.

From a distance, I paid attention to him that evening. I could tell just by looking at him that this was a man reflecting on his life, deep in thought. What was he thinking? I don't know but something was happening to me and, quite honestly, I was getting very nervous and uncomfortable with my own thoughts, considering where they had been in prior years when the image of Mel popped into my head.

But now my thoughts were not sexual in the least; I started to see the real man. I was taking notice of how he carried himself. Here was a man who had received devastating news, yet he was smiling, laughing, and walking with such dignity and courage. It was something I could not understand or put my finger on at the time. Why was I so intrigued with this man, this stranger? Why did I feel drawn to him? Why was I hoping I would somehow get the opportunity to invite this man into my life? What was happening to me? Where had my common sense gone? Why now, of all times, when I was considering making some pretty drastic changes in my own life was I so focused on this individual? I wanted to be on my own to figure out who I was and what I wanted out of life. I did not want anyone to be a part of it until I figured that out for myself. I actually thought I was starting to have a nervous breakdown. I was slowly driving myself crazy with my own thoughts about this stranger. I knew I would not be able to keep everything inside me for too much longer and would have to talk to someone about my situation. I needed help and I needed it now. I was so lost and it was starting to take its toll on me—not only mentally and emotionally, but physically as well.

But at this annual tournament, two months later, he looked fantastic. A picture of health, and that's what made it so hard to believe that this man had cancer. Perhaps a miracle had occurred and it was in remission. He was in his element when calling a game. How the players loved and respected him. Teams always wanted Mel as their umpire, especially if there was a lot riding on a particular game.

It was Saturday afternoon and I didn't have to play another game for a few hours. Dave was also between games when I bumped into him and, as usual, the jokes started flying between the two of us in no time. We were having a great time and then, surprisingly, Mel came to join in on the fun and laughter ... and I was officially introduced to Mel Malchuk.

It was at this weekend ball tournament that Mel and I actually had our first conversation. It was ten years in coming, and it was worth waiting for. The conversation flowed so easily between the two of us it was almost as though we had been friends forever. I felt so comfortable talking with him that I felt it was okay to ask him point blank questions about his cancer. I wanted to know how it was first detected, what he was feeling, what he was going through, what the prognosis was.

To my surprise, he was willing to share his thoughts with me. The thing that shook me to the core was that just by listening to the words roll off his tongue about life, experiences, dreams, mistakes, wants, and wishes, I was stimulated, mentally and intellectually. Deep-rooted honesty coming out about life, regrets, and the limited future made me see there was so much more to this man than mere physical beauty.

I now knew what the connection was for the two of us. We were both facing a death sentence—his was cancer, mine was a life sentence for a crime that I committed unknowingly. The big difference was that mine was curable while his was not. I had found someone with whom I could talk about life and other important and meaningful subjects. He would share some of his advice on what he felt was really important in life, especially now that his time was limited. What words of wisdom could he pass onto me that I could learn something from? During these conversations, I came to learn that this man had a personality, a sense of humour, wisdom, and a genuine sense of who he was. He, too, had come to terms with, and was starting to forgive himself for his past mistakes. I remember him telling me that weekend of the ball tournament that forgiveness is the key to living a happier life. He was so open and honest with his views on life. I found it so refreshingly beautiful to hear a man talk about such intimate and personal things, with no reservations. It was strange, but I remember thinking that even though our journeys took us down very different paths, we now seemed to be in the same place and were thinking along the same lines about the important things in life.

For the remainder of that weekend we would look for each other in the crowd to continue and pick up where we had left off in our last conversation. There was no denying it. There was an instant connection. It was like we were being pulled into something so much bigger than the two of us. By the end of that weekend I was sure of two things: I had just met and made a new friend, and I knew I was headed for trouble. I knew that it wouldn't be hard to fall in love with this man given the opportunity. I was no longer thinking with my head. I was thinking with my heart and listening to my inner voice.

During the remainder of that summer, Mel and I managed to innocently bump into each other. None of these encounters was pre-arranged. If we saw each other at a baseball diamond, it was a pleasant surprise. However, if I didn't see him in a particular week I felt that things were not complete. Something was missing. I was missing our talks. We were developing a very close, platonic relationship that summer and, the more time we spent together, the stronger those feelings became. He asked me why I was so interested in getting his advice on life lessons. What was I going through in my life to make me so inquisitive?

Mel knew that I was searching for answers but the questions seemed to interest him more. He was the first person I actually told that I was considering leaving my marriage. I was scared to death but knew that it was right for me because I had done so much soul searching and always came up with the same answer. I was finally able to tell someone my deep, dark secret and once the flood gates opened, there was no stopping the onslaught of words. I must have talked for hours on end about my situation, thoughts, dreams and reasons for leaving and, more importantly, why I felt there was no hope for repairing the mess I had made of things between Mark and me.

Mel had been married for over twenty years and the breakup was long in coming for him, as well. He could sympathize with my dilemma and totally understood my feelings of loneliness because he felt that too, near the end of his marriage. He asked if Mark and I had tried marriage counseling as an option, suggesting that talking to a third party might help our situation. When I told him I was frustrated with Mark not seeing that there was an issue with our marriage to begin with, I really started to question Mark's feelings about me. Why was he not able to see how unhappy I was, even after I told him that I felt something was missing? Why was it okay for me to do anything I wanted, with no questions asked? If he wanted to see how tormented and unhappy I was, all he had to do was really look at me, because the dramatic weight loss should have been an indication that something was terribly wrong with me. It just did not make sense to me. Why did he not want more from me? Why did he not want anything from me at all?

Mel and I talked about people growing apart and wanting different things in life. Was this a bad thing? I remember Mel saying that if a couple is not growing or learning from one another, or, more importantly, if there is loss of respect, it's a very hard situation to overcome. Respect for one another is critical. Wanting your partner to grow is essential and healthy.

After having many similar conversations with Mel over that summer, I knew something magical was happening between us.

We didn't dare tell each other how we felt because of both of our personal situations. If we said it out loud, it would become real and then what would we do? I knew my life was in shambles, that I had been struggling for quite some time, but was I about to add fuel to the fire and add Mel into the mix? Was Mel going to be the reason that would make me finally leave and uproot my life? Was Mel the purpose I had been searching for? Was this man meant to be in my life? So many questions, but no answers were presenting themselves to me and, yet, something was definitely pulling us toward each other.

The timing couldn't be worse, or was it the best timing? Mel's relationship, at the time of our meeting, had run its course and he was getting ready to leave, but then something happened to derail the plan—his terminal cancer diagnosis. He had to focus his energy on what mattered most, his life. We could not stop what was happening between us and the attraction was only intensifying. The more time we spent together talking about important issues, about the things that really mattered in life, the more I knew I had to have this man be a part of mine. I knew that I had met a man who was going to change my life forever. The only question was, was I going to let a little thing like cancer stand in the way of my happiness? Would I turn my back on the chance of experiencing true love in my life for the first time? Would I tell Mark that I was falling in love with another man I had only just met?

Things were getting complicated and messy, yet I was convinced there had to be a reason why the universe put Mel and me together. Why in the world would I be falling in love with a man who had just been diagnosed with terminal cancer? Why would Mel want to inject someone new into his life when the future held nothing for them? These were questions that we simply could not answer, except to say it is what it is.

Who said life is supposed to be easy anyway? This is the kind of thing that molds you, that makes you stronger and that defines you as a person and as a partner. Did we want to hurt others in the process of coming together as a couple? Of course not, but I knew beyond a shadow of a doubt that this relationship was meant to be. I don't know how it came to be. All I knew at the time was that I had asked the universe to give me a purpose in life, and Mel walked into it.

I told Mel I was falling in love with him, that I needed to be by his side for however long that would be. I was willing to take that risk. I told him that I would rather have a little bit of something with him than to never have anything with him at all. I believed at that moment that the universe was leading me right to Mel and Mel to me. When the student is ready, the teacher will appear.

Later on in our relationship, Mel and I would joke about this from time to time. He would ask, "Kim, who do you think is going to be the teacher today, you or me?" We would just laugh, because it didn't matter. We both knew that the lessons we would teach each other would help us grow spiritually, emotionally, physically, and mentally.

I was absolutely sure that I would love this man for however long we were given. What was even clearer, because I had a sense inside me that I could not ignore, we were going to be given time. The universe would make that happen for us, so in the fall of 1999 I made some serious changes to share that time with Mel. I walked into this situation with my eyes wide open. I promised myself I would never let cancer stand in the way of this relationship. I also knew that if we continued to see each other, and I was not prepared to end the relationship anytime soon, I wasn't sure how much longer I could continue to honour my wedding vows.

I wanted to get lost in this man. I chose to leave my marriage before this beautiful partnership Mel and I were developing could turn into something sneaky and wrong. There was nothing wrong with the love I felt for him. I also chose to leave my career behind, because climbing the corporate ladder was no longer important to me. I needed to work, but I would find another job that would give me back my personal time. Life is just too short to be spending valuable time in an office when you could be in the arms of someone who makes your world worth living for. I was gaining perspective on what and who was important in my life. I was learning to set my priorities. I finally understood there are more important things in life than being a successful career woman. I chose to stand by Mel's side and I chose not to listen to what the doctors said about the prognosis, because we were going to beat this thing and we were going to do it together. I was not going to play in the cancer game. I would play in the game of life and live it one day at a time. I wouldn't think about the future. I would focus on the now and on both of us. If we could do that with both of our hearts, honestly and freely, we would be given the time to learn our life lessons from one another. I was sure of it.

With this knowledge and commitment, I had made a personal spiritual agreement with the universe: to love Mel with all of me and never hold anything back. Mel couldn't believe my determination, energy, and positive outlook on how we were going to move forward. My energy lifted Mel up and, for the first time since being diagnosed, he was excited at the possibility of kicking the crap out of cancer, having a reason to live life, and doing it with someone who truly loved and believed in him.

Love is passionate and at times a little obsessive. You know that you are loved when you have loved like a crazy person. And what's even better is when you get that same kind of love back. You never tire of seeing each other. You yearn to be by each other's side always, yet you know the importance of independence and what that does for self-image and growth. It can only benefit the couple as a whole. You learn how self-satisfying it is to put someone else's needs before your own. You become selfless. You are a couple, yet you never lose yourself or your identity because your partner will not allow that to happen to you. You come to finally understand what God, Buddha, Mohammed, Oprah *(whoever it is you believe in)* mean by "Love is the only answer."

The most valuable life lesson I have ever learned is that of love—unconditional love. I am so grateful that I took the risk and made the choice to invite that kind of "crazy" love into my life. I was beginning to understand what it meant to be a partner, and it was wonderful to finally feel what it was like to be needed, to truly matter to someone. I made a difference in someone's life and it came just at the right time—for both of us.

Maybe God wants us to meet a few wrong people before meeting the right one so that when we finally do meet that person we will treasure and treat him or her as a precious gift. The universe delivered, as it always does, and I am forever grateful to it.

Chapter Three

Welcome Home

In June 2000, Mel and I became an official couple. When the dust settled on both sides, we could not wait for the day that we could begin to wake up every morning by each other's side, but we also had to be realists. Time was not on our side and we definitely wanted to take full advantage of every day we were given. We had already wasted ten months, but no more. We were together at last and it felt so right. The only thing missing now was a child.

Children! I had been so adamant that I didn't want children. No way. Never! Not going to do it. Then I welcomed Mel into my life. We had a long, heart-to-heart talk. What if I got pregnant? Would that be so terrible? We actually toyed with that idea and said hey, if it happens it happens. Then one night Mel sat me down and said he just couldn't do it. It was bad enough that he was already being selfish by loving me and letting me into his life when the conditions were not working in our favour. He had to live with that thought, that decision, which, at times, he admitted, nearly drove him crazy. Now, we bring a baby into the picture?

Tears were welling up in his eyes when he said, "I can't continue to do this, Kim. I will not bring a child into this world for it to never know its father and for you to be burdened with raising a child all on your own, especially this late in your life."

After he said that, there was no need to talk anymore. The decision had been made. No more words were needed.

One of the most beautiful memories I have of us is from that time. We were acting like we were in our late twenties, early thirties. Why shouldn't we entertain the idea of having children? It astonishes me when I look back to when we first started out. I was almost forty and Mel was almost fifty but we were both acting like we were childhood sweethearts. What a fantastic feeling! But we could not have gotten together at a worse time in Mel's medical life if we had tried. The odds were so stacked against us—against our time together. To get through this and to simply enjoy the time that we did have, we chose not to acknowledge Mel's cancer. We would not allow ourselves to focus or dwell on it. In fact, we did such a good job of ignoring the illness that there were many times I had to remind myself that Mel actually had terminal cancer; I simply forgot. We were completely wrapped up in the feelings of each day and of each other. We were living in the now. We didn't want to rush through any day for fear of missing out on the hidden treasure that might be there waiting for us to discover. We welcomed the next day with open arms. We honoured each new day that was given to us to explore, to learn, love, laugh, and to share with one another. We never took the day for granted and we lived each one grateful and thankful.

That was how we turned a three-month death sentence into five and half years of some pretty amazing and wonderful experiences that are mine to treasure forever. I am convinced that the combination of positive attitude, being grateful for every day, laughing and loving put cancer into remission for so many years. If you or someone you love is ever faced with terrible news that your life is coming to an abrupt end, I urge you to live each day to the fullest and enjoy all you have. Surround yourself with people and events that make your heart sing. Travel, laugh, love and appreciate each day that is given to you, because it is truly a gift. Prioritize what is really important to you. You will be amazed at what that kind of attitude and thinking can bring into your life. It brings you time.

I wouldn't acknowledge or focus on cancer, and Mel thrived because of it. His doctors were amazed at his progress when the original diagnosis had been so dismal. There is definitely something to be said about having a positive attitude when it comes to health issues. It can make a life or death difference.

Over the years, we took advantage of our independence and traveled to hot spots during the winter months. The summer months were reserved for our two loves: baseball and camping. The greatest gift Mel shared with me was his love of nature, the outdoors. If we were not involved with a baseball event on the weekend, that Friday evening after work, I would come home and Mel would have the camper all packed and ready to roll. How we loved hitting the highway in the camper, our paradise on wheels.

Our weekends would consist of barbecuing meals fit for royalty, fishing all day and, perhaps, a little during some early evenings, playing cards or board games while listening to great music until the sun was coming up. Making love where and whenever we wanted to. We were always a little disappointed when Sunday afternoon snuck up on us. We knew that we would have to start packing up, disassembling our site, and start heading back to the city, another beautiful weekend come to an end. Why couldn't we just make time stand still? The disappointment, however, would fade quickly, because on the drive home Mel would turn to me and ask, "So where should we go next weekend?"

Even our everyday life at home was precious to us. We were happy to watch TV together or entertain family and friends. That was a common event at our home. Mel loved to cook; it was his way of showing his love for those close to us. The special people in our lives would never pass up a meal made by Mel. He was a phenomenal cook and an even better baker. It was amazing to see this masculine man cooking up a storm in the kitchen and, to be honest with you, it was quite the turn-on. I mean, come on, what woman doesn't love the idea of a man knowing his way around a kitchen? That was the thing about Mel. He was just as comfortable in the kitchen with an apron tied around his mid-drift as he was fixing his truck or gutting a deer. He was so confident in everything he did and I found that quality so attractive.

It wasn't too long after Mel and I were finally moved in and settled into the condo that I realized that we had made a home. That may sound strange to you, but when that feeling came over me, I knew we were meant to be exactly where we were at that exact moment. You see, I had never experienced that feeling in my first marriage. I lived in a house and that's how I felt. I didn't know there was a difference. Do you? There is a huge difference between living in a house and living in a home. A house is just that, a roof over your head, a place to sleep, eat and bathe.

As for a home, well, a home is something completely different. It's warm and inviting. It's lived in and messed up. It has aromas coming from the kitchen that leave your mouth watering. It's filled with laughter and so much love that when visitors come over, they don't know why but they just never want to leave—not yet anyway, "Let's just stay a little bit longer," I would often hear our guests say.

This was a gift we gave to one another and experienced it for the first time in each of our lives. We both knew we had a strong foundation for our new home. Our home was built on love and there was nothing—not even a little disease called cancer—that could knock our home off its foundation. It was just too strong. Nothing could bring it down.

The years that followed were pretty much the same. We travelled, entertained, loved all the time, ate and drank like kings, and had secret little getaways. At the same time, we had the odd doctor's appointment and test that interrupted our busy schedule of life.

But cancer was not going to occupy our thoughts or slow us down. I was not going to let this thing win and take away what I had waited for all my adult life. Mel's doctor was amazed at how well he responded to new, experimental drugs, different therapies, or nothing at all. As you can imagine, over the years, you develop relationships with doctors and nurses whom you are seeing on a regular basis. We had become very close with Mel's oncologist's head nurse, Kathy. Talk about an earthly angel. She was a godsend to us. I remember her saying that she felt Mel was doing so well because of our love for each other and, most importantly, our positive attitude toward life. This was coming from a woman who deals with death every single day when she goes to work.

She said she could immediately pick out the people who are not going to make it. Once they have heard the news, that's it for them! They give up, and what is even sadder, the person that they would lean on for support gives up right along with them because they cannot imagine a life without their loved one. She not only knew that Mel was going to kick the crap out of cancer, but that he had his own personal cheerleader in his corner—me. We were not going to lie down and let this disease take over our lives without a good fight. We still had too much living to do and were not going to waste a minute of it.

When Mel and I agreed to take the risk of starting our relationship, there was something very odd between the two of us that was never verbalized, yet very much understood. We promised each other to live one day at a time and not focus on the future, to enjoy what we had today. Should the universe offer us a tomorrow—then we would welcome it with joy and gratitude. We never dwelled on the past and, strangely enough, neither one of us talked about the distant future. The only time that we would do anything that was future-oriented was when we were planning our winter vacations.

I will let you in on a little secret. I was scared that if I even thought about the future with Mel, everything would be jinxed and the universe would say to me, *"Kim, you reneged on your deal with me. You told me that you would live for today and not focus on the future with this man and, in turn, I would give you time with him. Now that you have gone back on your word to me, what do you think I should do?"*

Can you see the reasoning behind that kind of thinking? I didn't want to tempt fate. I had already been given years with Mel by sticking to my original, spiritual contract that I made with the universe, so why rock the boat? Don't be greedy, Kim. Just stick to your plan of living for the day that you have been given. Live up to your promises and be true to them. Treat life as the gift that it is. If you do that, the universe will give you more of what you are experiencing in that moment. Everything and anything you truly want will be yours, if it comes from your heart.

So you can imagine my surprise when Mel asked me to marry him. This, coming from a man who said he would never get married again. We didn't talk future, so we never really talked about marriage all that much. Oh sure, we joked about it from time to time, saying that we both had been married before and look how well we did with that. Why would we go and ruin our relationship by getting married, when it didn't work the first time for either one of us?

The truth for me was that a piece of paper and a ring weren't going to make one bit of difference in my heart. I already felt as though we were living together as husband and wife. We were partners and in this life together. I could not believe how much life we had lived in those first two years and how much I had grown personally in our relationship. I liked, and more importantly, I loved the person who was staring back at me from the mirror. That person was softer, kinder, and so filled with love. I felt like I was floating rather than walking through life. I was where I was supposed to be. We both were.

Before Mel had come into my life, I lived my life very stringently. Things were either black or white, right or wrong—nothing in between. I was so stubborn and set in my ways that I wouldn't bend. I was never wrong. It had to be my way or no way at all. Then Mel came into my life and that life was filled vibrant colours. I was with a partner who challenged me and told me things like, *"Being right all the time or being the best is no way to live. It's too stressful and takes so much energy out of you. Listen to others and be open-minded about what they say—you might learn something new if you really listen. You don't have to agree with them or with me for that matter, but don't shut people out or view them as stupid because they happen not to agree with you."*

We lived a very simple life and because of that our everyday life seemed lighter. We were not carrying the weight of the world on our shoulders and this afforded us the opportunity to enjoy our lives and our home. I had never felt so "at home" as I did in those first few years with Mel. I felt as though we had been together for many years, but always remained in the honeymoon stage. I remember thinking how sad it was that I had never felt this connection, this bond with Mark, even after eleven years of marriage.

Early fall was our favourite time of the year. The leaves on the trees are starting to turn into golden yellows and brilliant reds. The temperature is cool enough that you can wear only a thin jacket or sweater. The mosquitoes are long gone so you can go for long walks without being pestered.

On September 9, 2002, after having one of Mel's fabulous

meals, he asked me out on a date. Would I like to accompany him on the back of his motorcycle and take advantage of the beautiful evening offered to us and go wherever the road would take us? I, of course, said yes because Mel would be putting the motorcycle away for another year in just a couple of weeks. We put our gear on, jumped on the bike and were on our way. He asked where I wanted to go and I told him to surprise me.

We ended up on the outskirts of the city at a place many out-of-towners visit during the summer months because of the beautiful and quiet surroundings. When we arrived, it was a little eerie to see that no one else was at the park. We walked over to a bench and sat down to soak in the sights. This park overlooks our city's lock and dam, and, on this particular night, there were many boats out on the water taking advantage of the beautiful weather.

We were sitting there when Mel asked me, as I was looking out at the boaters, what I was thinking about at that very moment. I started to giggle and said, "Do you really want to know? I was thinking that this night could not be more perfect. The only thing missing is you getting down on one knee and asking me to marry you. We are the only people here and it feels like you made a special reservation just for tonight. There. That's what I am thinking." Why I said that, I had no clue, but there it was.

He started to laugh and then was trying to get something out of his rainpants pocket. I turned the other way to continue looking at the boats, giggling about what I had just told him. He asked me to look back at him and when I did, he was holding a ring box in his hand. Talk about ruining a surprise. We both laughed until we cried. I apologized for taking away his moment, but he didn't care. He got down on one knee and asked if I would marry him. I was both thrilled and shocked at the same time.

I asked him, "Why the change of heart?" He said, "I never imagined love could feel this way. Even though we know how important we are to each other, I want the world to know I have found my soul mate. You are more than just a girlfriend, lover and friend. You are my life but, more importantly, you have given me a second chance to live my life."

Tears were running down my face as I accepted his proposal. I hadn't ruined everything that night. Mel walked back to his bike, opened the saddlebag, pulled out a bottle of champagne, along with two plastic champagne flutes. We toasted to the day, to ourselves, and, to second chances.

We wanted our wedding to be something very small and simple. We wanted only close friends and family present to share in the exchanging of our vows. We ended up getting married at an establishment that was so fitting for us as a couple, it almost screamed out to us when we drove up to scout it out as a possible venue for our upcoming nuptials. It was just outside the city limits yet gave you the feeling you were hundreds of miles away. It was a beautiful, rustic, country house converted into a very quaint restaurant that had received glowing reviews from city food critics touting the talents of the chef. We knew the instant we drove up, without even having to taste the delicious meal that was about to be prepared for us, that this was the place.

We got married on the evening of December 28, 2002. Our winters can be terribly cold, unpredictable, and it would not be unrealistic at that time of year for temperatures to be -35 to -40 Celsius with the wind chill. But that was not going to happen and it never even entered our minds. Mel and I were convinced that we were going to have a beautiful evening. We just knew everything was going to be fine.

Sure enough, the evening could not have been more perfect. We drove up and saw the house for the first time in the evening. Thousands and thousands of tiny white lights were strung throughout not only the house itself, but also along the pathway that leads from the parking lot all the way to the house. The railing along that pathway was lit, as were all the trees in the yard.

With all the fresh snow that fell during the day it was a Currier and Ives Christmas card come to life, and, we were the magical couple illustrated on the front of it. It was beautiful beyond my wildest dreams. There was such stillness that night. I felt that there was an invisible shield surrounding and protecting our wedding haven for the evening. Some of our guests commented that the day was truly blessed by God to have turned out so unseasonably warm.

The entire evening was intimate and elegant. Many of our guests commented on how beautiful and delicious, warm and romantic it was, how they would never forget how special the evening was for them as well as for us. They witnessed a couple blessed with a second chance at life and at love.

What do you do when you are given a second chance? Do you take full advantage of correcting or at least not repeating what you did the first time around? Sometimes we do and sometimes we don't. I will give you an example of what I mean.

Have you ever heard yourself say, "Why does this always happen to me?"

Kiminition: on that question:

When we find ourselves in the same situation time and time again, when a lesson is being offered to us repeatedly, it's because we have not learned the lesson set before us. That same lesson will keep reappearing because you are asking the universe for a second chance to get it right. So what does the universe do? It gives you more of the same of what you are asking for until you get it right and achieve a different outcome. This situation will stop appearing once you quit asking for it, because you feel as though you got it right.

But how do we get a different outcome to move past these recurring situations? We make a different choice. We stop repeating our old habits when faced with that same situation for a second, third or fourth time. It gives a whole new meaning to that saying "old habits die hard", wouldn't you say?

Some of us are quick studies and learn from having the experience only once, so that we can pass the test set before us and move on to others. We call those people high achievers. Then there are the majority of people who messed up the first time and ask the universe for another chance to get it right. The universe delivers and they make different choices to get a better and different outcome the second time around.

And then there are those of us who need to have the experience presented time and time again. We call those people stubborn, set in their ways, addicted to certain emotions or, simply, special. In all scenarios, it's a matter of time until we decide to start making different choices. Then the situation will stop repeating itself.

When Mel came into my life I made the choice to work on the things that I felt I had done wrong with Mark, so that I would get a different outcome. I also chose to redefine my ideals about marriage and what it meant to me.

How was I going to be a better partner, a better wife the second time around? Well, the first thing I was going to do was to be an active participant. I was not going to be a silent partner. If I didn't like something I would say so, but if I liked something I would say it even louder so that my partner would know. I would constantly be communicating with my partner not expecting him to read my mind. I would put my heart and soul into making the relationship work. I would put that person at the forefront every time.

When I decided to leave my career behind and find a regular job, I did so because I learned that there are more important things in life than having a big pay cheque. A high-paying position comes with a high price. It usually requires a person to put in longer hours, travel, and sometimes manage staff. All of this is fine, if it's what you truly want. But you must realize that it comes with sacrifices that usually end up taking away personal time, which will have a negative impact on your home situation.

You can't always be home at 5 p.m. every day so supper will get cold; or worse, you find yourself eating more meals alone.

You might be bringing work home with you in the evenings because you just never had the chance to get the task done during the day, because of constant interruptions or problems with your staff. You may have to be away from home to attend meetings, or perhaps you might have to slip into the office on the odd Saturday to get a head start on the upcoming week. You may have to give up family/friend events because something has detained you, yet again, at the office. This is all fine, but it will eventually take its toll on the relationship.

I had to prioritize the things that were important to me in order to be the partner I wanted to be. My time with Mel took priority above everything else. I was not going to repeat my old work habits and take time away from Mel like I did when I was married to Mark. Work is just that. It's a job and your spouse/partner should never take a backseat to it.

That's another important lesson I learned about a career versus a job. I have experienced both and prefer to have a normal work/life balance at this stage in my life and will never go back to the long managerial hours. Life is too short to spend it working yourself to death or out of a relationship. Your partner deserves more than that because this is the person who agreed to care for and to love you and, really, what has your job promised you? Nothing—except a paycheque.

Mel saw how dedicated I was to making our relationship work and, because of that, he knew he truly mattered to me. He was my reason for getting up every day and rushing home at the end of every work day just to be by his side again. When you are in a relationship, give it all you have or get out. If you are truly giving all of you to the relationship, your partner will feed off it and reciprocate. What you give is what you get back, I kid you not.

Mel told me many times that when he saw me look at him he could feel the love pouring out of my eyes without my mouth uttering the words, "I love you." And because of that, he was finally able to allow love into his life for the first time and give it back freely with absolutely no hesitation. We both wanted to ensure that we got it right this time around, that we made sure that we did not repeat the same mistakes made in both of our pasts. We did not want our pasts to interfere with our now or with our future. When we saw each other sliding into our old habits, we called each other on it so that we could make different choices about how to better handle a situation. This is how you grow as a couple, but you have to have a safe environment, one based on respect, honesty and communication. You learn to really listen to what the other person is saying and allow them to convey what they are feeling without placing any judgment or holding it against them for speaking their truth. Once that safety net is in place and you feel yourself falling from time to time, and you will, you know that you will never hit the ground, because someone will always be there to catch you.

When I redefined my views on marriage I quickly realized how wonderful it was to have someone look after me and, even better, how satisfying it was to look after someone else. I learned how to put someone else's needs before my own. I stopped being selfish in my ways. I know this may sound odd to you, but I could almost feel myself growing because of it. This kind of consideration was new to me and I really liked the feeling. I felt that I was needed and that made me feel special in a way that I had never experienced until then. It gave me a sense of importance, of value.

Now, there is a huge difference between being needed and being dependent. Dependent means that you are helpless in a situation. When someone is needed, they know they are valued and appreciated for what they contribute to the partnership. You are partners and in the relationship together, so it's more than acceptable to help each other out whenever needed. It isn't a sign of weakness—quite the opposite. It brings a couple closer together because you feel more connected and that makes the partnership that much stronger. You matter to that person, and you are in this together as equals.

Isn't that really the reason why two people marry in the first place? I mean, if we didn't want that type of caring and sharing, then we should never have gotten married. We should have just lived alone and continued to do things for ourselves and remained single. When you marry, you have to give up part of your independence because now there are two of you; there is someone else to take into consideration. That can be a very difficult adjustment to make; I know this to be true because I am speaking from my experience with Mark.

I was not prepared to give up my independence when Mark and I married, because I thought that was a sign of weakness. My job at the time of our marriage was one in which I was constantly making decisions, in charge, and calling all the shots. Unfortunately that flowed over into our marriage. Mark, on the other hand, was very passive and allowed it to happen because he wanted to make me happy and he played the role of the "really nice guy". I don't blame him for that, because he did what he thought was the best at the time for the both of us.

But what happened over time was that I was sick of making decisions at work and just wanted someone else to make them for me at home. I was tired of always being the strong one and longed for someone to look after me for once. I wore the pants in that family and took full advantage of it.

When I was not getting any pushback from Mark, my independence only got stronger, but then something very dangerous happened. I ended up losing respect for Mark because he allowed me to get away with my holier-than-thou attitude for far too long. I could do anything I wanted to with no repercussions. That is just not right, especially when you are in a relationship. I am sure that the reason Mark never complained about our situation was because he knew he had given me all the power in that relationship long ago. We played by my rules, and if Mark had tried to establish some new rules late in the game, I am not sure how well that would have played out. I think we both knew it would have been disastrous.

When one person has all the power, the relationship is destined to fail. You have to be in it together—fifty/fifty. You have to be able to come into a committed relationship knowing that it cannot always be your way. You will have to make concessions every once in a while and know that it is okay to do so. It's a give-and-take relationship. That was where Mel and I really gelled as a couple. Mel would never let me get away with that kind of conduct and I would never have attempted it with him, because I saw him as my equal. You teach people how to treat you. He had a voice in the relationship and was not afraid to use it, and I would never stifle his words, nor would he stifle mine. I valued, respected and looked forward to hearing his views and ideas. I was thrilled that I had someone in my life to help me make decisions. It was a partnership based on respect, trust and equality. We made decisions together. That was what made our house a home and our marriage a working partnership.

Chapter Four

Something Has Changed

In 2004, our relationship was tested to the core or, I should say, I was tested. Did I mean everything I said to Mel in front of our close family and friends when we exchanged marriage vows? Was I as strong as I proclaimed to be all these years? I would find out sooner than I expected. We both had been living the last four and half years in positive denial. We had beaten this thing— we were so sure of it—and then, suddenly, Mel was acting differently. He was quiet, more reflective, and a bit distant. He seemed to be miles away from me at times. When I would ask where he was, he would simply brush it off so that I wouldn't worry. He was trying to shield me from something he didn't want me to know and didn't want me to see. That was Mel, my protector, my warrior, but it was too late.

For the first time since we had been together, something inside of me knew that our time was coming to an end, but I dared not say a word to anyone for fear saying it out loud would be admitting defeat. So I kept quiet, yet I knew I would have to talk to somebody about my thoughts and fears. Who could I talk to about this? Mel had been my confidant, so who could I turn to now? Was I reading too much into Mel's demeanour or was this the beginning of the end for us?

If I truly wanted answers to those questions, all I had to do was take note and pay close attention to Mel's actions. He had turned to another source for reassurance, to the highest source some might say. He was reading the Bible on a more frequent basis, something I had never seen him do before. It gave him comfort and relief in ways I knew I never could. I had not taken the time to sit down and seriously read the Bible because it scared me and, quite frankly, I wasn't sure I believed in God. I knew that I believed in a higher power, but what or who that was, well, let's just say I am still trying to figure that one out. All I know for sure is that I do believe and I think that's the most important thing.

Kiminition: on religion:

Messages are so mixed up and the rules are really hard to live by and, God forbid, you dare make a mistake. Even though you are trying to live a good and honest life, God doesn't forgive you for ever stumbling along the way. He also has this incredible memory, so he never forgets who messed up, and according to the readings and scriptures if you do not live by God's rules, well sorry to say, you will be punished no matter what.

I was so confused because what about the God who grants us free will? What about the God who will always love me, no matter what? What about the God who is supposed to be an all-forgiving God? What about all of that? That's the God I want to meet and hang out with for all of eternity, if he really does exist. That's my Father who is out there in heaven (Hallowed be Thy name), not the one the church and religious zealots are describing most of the time.

Instead of putting the fear of God into me, they actually put the fear of God out of me, and made me stay away from church altogether. Why would I want to get up early every Sunday morning to go and see the "bogeyman"?

For those reasons, and much more, I am disillusioned with, and leery of organized religion. I think our church leaders have done a really bad job of getting God's messages out, especially for those who really want to believe in something greater than themselves, but who find the rules just too hard to live by. Then what happens? People start to lose faith in themselves because of the mistakes they have made in their journey and fear that they have really ticked him off. So then they give up.

Well, my belief is that this greater power just wants us to learn from our mistakes, grow from the risks that we take and do the best we can. It was during this time, when Mel's health was worsening, that I finally understood that there is a huge difference between religion and spirituality. There just might be hope for me after all because this higher power can see that I am really trying hard to just be the best that I can be. Do your best and you will be rewarded, I am sure of that.

So there I was—a non-religious person needing some help, some guidance to get me through this next chapter in both of our lives. I had never been this close and personal with death before. I didn't know how to act, what to say, and I didn't even know how to pray. How could I not show Mel that on the inside I was crumbling like a house of cards, but show him on the outside that I was a tower of strength for him to lean on should he need to.

I sat back and thought about the lesson Mel was teaching me during this time. I remembered that every time he had finished reading some scripture from the Bible, there was a sense of calmness and peace within him. He even spoke differently—more from the heart, with more meaning and feeling than ever before. We never talked about why, after all of those years, Mel had turned to the Bible for answers. It didn't matter; we both knew why. It was a choice that Mel made for himself and something that he was not going to hide from me or be embarrassed about. He was preparing himself for the end. He was reacquainting himself with the words of God, from when he was a little boy, so that he could come to understand and get answers to the questions that I am sure he was asking this higher power.

Because of this example, I, too, made the choice to put aside all of my fears, doubts, pre-conceived ideas about God, religion and church and simply ask this higher power or the universe to give me the strength, courage and dignity to move forward. The universe was there for me before when it presented Mel to me, so now, if I called upon it, perhaps it would be there for me again, listening to my prayers and giving me answers. This was the time, purely out of fear, desperation and love, that I would turn to that higher power and really demand some action, some direction. It was as if I was going to test the whole "higher power" issue to find out for myself, once and for all, if it really did exist.

Would Higher Power really be there for me going forward if I truly asked for its guidance and encouragement to help get me through this? I wanted to find my spiritual path and I needed to do it quickly. If Mel was getting answers and comfort from the Bible, then perhaps there was something in there for me as well. I just had to go with an open mind and let myself believe that, when needed, HP would be there for me as well, be it in spirit, signs or the written word.

I finally got my answer to an earlier question. Who was I going to talk to about all of this? I knew that over the next while I would be having my own personal, heart-to-heart conversations with HP on a more regular basis. HP was going to be my conduit so that I could have a way to safely confide my deepest hopes and fears, without being judged.

But now, would I even know how to talk to HP? Would I talk to HP like I would a friend? Would I have to address HP in a certain way, so that He/She knows I'm really serious and need help this time, as opposed to the last time I asked for assistance, when the jackpot for the national lottery was in the millions?

I was confused about how I was going to channel my prayers, hopes and dreams to HP, but I knew one thing for sure. I would be listening to my inner voice, my higher self, more than ever before. I thought that if this HP truly existed and was there to help me, it would communicate to me through my inner voice.

Now was going to be the time to live up to the promises I had made to Mel and, most importantly, to myself. To love this man until the end of time and, unfortunately, I knew in my heart, that that time was slowly creeping up on us. I had to remember who I was and how far I had come on this journey with Mel. If I reflected on how I got to this point, I would know how to proceed and be the partner my husband needed me to be, to be the partner I wanted to be for him.

What did my past teach me and what had I learned from living in the now so that I could face the inevitable—a life without Mel? When I left Mark, I chose to discard all the negatives in my life—my marriage, some of my friends, his family, my house, my possessions and my career—to start all over again to have a better and happier life. I made the choice to change my outlook and thoughts. I had to change my reality because what you project is what you attract and I no longer wanted what I was attracting into my life back then.

Long before any of us had heard about the book entitled *The Secret,* (for those of you unfamiliar with this book, written by Rhonda Byrne, I will touch on it in Chapter 11) there was an actual name for this phenomenon. It's called the Law of Attraction. You get what you reap. Ask and you shall receive. Your wish is my command. I knew all those years ago what can happen to a life when you choose to live with negative thoughts and bitterness all the time. The universe will continue to give you more of the same because it cannot differentiate between good and bad, positive and negative. It just knows to continue to keep on giving you more of the same.

Progress can never be achieved without change. If everything stays the same, how can it physically get better or improve? It's metabolically impossible. In order to evolve, a change has to occur. So when I decided to take a second chance at life and put my past lessons learned into practice, I promised myself to not ever surround myself with negative thoughts, people or situations going forward. Keep the drama out of my life as much as I possibly could.

One of the biggest lessons I learned living life with Mel, and continue to practice today, is that a simple life is a better life. Living a life without stress is healthy. It allows you to grow and flourish as an individual. You are open and ready to receive the gifts the universe will lay before you.

I truly believe that my positive outlook on life while at Mel's side gave us time. He fed off my energy to keep cancer at bay and, at the same time, I had grown as an individual and was finally able to see the beauty that life has to offer everyone. Living in a positive state allowed me to let my inner light shine and, when I did that, I gave Mel permission to do the same. I am positive this radiance helped prolong his life.

The power of our thoughts is incredible. Change your thoughts and you change your life. I will say it over and over again—thoughts (yours and mine) are so very powerful. Here's a strong example to prove my point. When I noticed a change in Mel's health and could sense his worries, I allowed fear and doubt to enter my thoughts. That's where I feel that I made a really bad choice. I chose negative thinking over positive for the first time since being together. I gave into my fears and into his. Where did all my good thoughts go? They stood by me for many years, so why did they decide to leave me now?

From my past lessons I should know better because I should have known what can happen when you think negatively. The universe will deliver. It wasn't that my good thoughts just up and left my mind, it's that I chose to let the negative thoughts in and focused on them, rather than on the positive. We both did.

Today, nobody could ever convince me or shake my belief

system when it comes to choosing to live each day positively as opposed to negatively. Our story is living proof of what can happen when you choose positive. Positive wins every single time. We never gave cancer a seat at the dinner table. Cancer was an uninvited guest who had no place in our home. We simply focused on the now, the day, each other, laughing, playing, and then appreciated the stillness, the quiet times, the simple times, and nature. We took the time to appreciate all the small things in life. We went back to the basics of life. Material things were not important to us, and living that way gave us five years longer than any of the doctors said Mel was ever going to have. But the minute we both lost our way and started to let our fears guide our thoughts, we had only months. That is how quickly the universe can respond to negative thoughts.

So I ask you now, how powerful do you think your thoughts are and, if you change your thoughts, can you really change your life? Napoleon Hill stated, "Life reflects your own thoughts back to you," and I couldn't agree more. Our situation was living proof of that.

I received an email from one of my "earthly angels" about a year ago. I am so grateful that this angel is part of my life, and how lucky am I that she happens to be my oldest sister, Rose? Some angels we can see but most of them we can't, but they are here for us nonetheless.

Rose is definitely one of my angels whom I treasure and cherish, because she always makes me feel that I really matter and that the world is a better place because I am in it. She plays many roles in my life. She is not only my sister, but also the mother I did not have, my cheerleader and, best of all, she is my best friend.

You might recognize the name of the email that Rose sent me, because in this day and age news travels very fast via the Internet. It was called, "A Reason, a Season or a Lifetime". We are living in an era of excess—to the point of disgust in some cases. *(I will not go on about that here. I might later on, but not right now.)*

My point is that sometimes really important messages get lost in the shuffle of life. We are so busy keeping busy, doing busy, living busy that we are actually missing out on something pretty extraordinary—our life and the messages the universe is trying to give us. It goes by way too quickly. In a flash we take notice and wonder where it all went.

When I decided to leave Mark and start a new life for myself all those years ago, not only did I decide to live a more positive life but I also chose to live an un-busy life. Make time for what is important, jump off the corporate ladder, leave all the office politics behind the door and just get a normal nine-to-five job. I wanted, at the end of each work day, to be excited about being at home with a person who makes me feel that I matter, to know that I make a difference in his world and that I am appreciated for what and who shows up in our relationship.

I am so grateful that I still, to this day, live an un-busy life, because if I had not continued to live this way I probably would have junked Rose's email and lost the importance of its message. The message helped me understand and become clearer about the people who come in and out of our lives. We hear it so often when talking to a friend or a family member who has suffered a lost relationship. That dreaded question we have all been asked by the person who is deeply hurting, "Why did they leave me, why did this have to happen to me?"

After reading the message from this particular email, which has stayed with me, the next time I am asked that question, I will be so much better prepared with my answer instead of my normal canned response of, *"because they're an idiot and they don't know what they have thrown away."*

No! No more! My answer will simply be "because they filled their role in the story of your life. They are just one within a cast of many who will come and go and play a part in it."

I am paraphrasing the contents of the email but it goes very much along these lines. The people who come into our lives for a Reason usually come to fill a need, a desire, or they are the answer to a prayer we have sent up to God. They seem like a godsend at the time, and they truly are, for God has sent them to us, but only for a short time. They were never meant to be in our lives for very long because once their job is done our need is fulfilled and it is time for them to move on.

The people who come into our life for a Season? Well, now it's our turn to share, grow and learn. They bring incredible happiness into our life and make us laugh. They may teach us something we never knew before, but only for a season.

Then there are those who come into our lives for a Lifetime. Those relationships teach you lifetime lessons so that you can build upon them and have a more solid and emotional foundation. Your job is to accept those lessons, love that person and then put what you have learned to use in all of your other relationships and areas of your life going forward.

Do I even have to tell you what Mel was to me? I will never forget the first time I told Mel that I knew it to be my truth that I loved him with all of my heart and soul. We were about three months into our relationship. He had been in Washington for tests. I was anxiously awaiting his arrival at the airport. Talking to him over the phone during that week was great, but I missed him so much I couldn't wait to take him back to my place so that we could get lost in each other. I remember looking into his beautiful blue eyes and I said that for the first time in my life, at the age of thirty-seven, I truly knew what it meant to be in love. His response filled me with such peacefulness that I was at a complete loss for words. I was lying in his arms and he immediately said to me, "Do you know what's even better for me Kim? I know that I am in love for the very first and last time in my life."

In order to make sense of why people are sometimes taken away from us far too early in life, here is my Kiminition about all of us being eternal beings and how we agreed to come to Earth to experience an earthly existence:

When we were hanging out in the eternal world together and decided to come down to Earth, we signed up for the era we would choose to live in during that earthly life and, more importantly, the people who were going to share in the experience. I will give you an example that might help illustrate what I mean so that you do not think I have completely lost my mind. Have you ever met someone with whom there was an instant connection, and the bond you felt with them was unbreakable? You say to yourself, it's like that person and I have always known each other. They totally get me. They are like the brother, sister, mother, father, lover, husband or wife you never had. Well, guess what? You most likely were eternal soul mates in paradise, hovering around, having a blast and causing nothing but trouble. You and these other souls made a pact that when on Earth, you would meet again some day.

I believe that is how it happened for Mel and me because of the instant bond we had. Mel and I agreed we would meet each other in this earthly life at the exact moment we did. It was part of the master plan. It was all pre-determined. We were soul mates in the eternal world and we were going to be the same here on Earth and in our other lives to come. I believe that as sure as I am breathing at this moment. We all decided when our ultimate departure date will be and what the circumstances will be long before we got here.

Mel decided that his fate would be cancer, but that before he left he would get the chance to experience love for the first and last time as the greatest parting gift ever. In return, he would teach me many life lessons so that I would be able to go forward on the remainder of my journey as a better person and partner. This is what I believe and what has allowed me to get through hard times so that I can make sense of it all.

The night I told Mel that I was positive I was in love with

him, I remember also saying, *"Wouldn't it be wonderful to be able to bottle this feeling and sell it to everyone? For everyone in the entire universe to feel what we feel at this very moment. If we could do that, we would be rich beyond our wildest dreams."*

Just imagine our planet filled with people who love each other like that. No more wars, unrest, genocides, power struggles between countries, starvation and homelessness. There would be no such thing as better or worse—it would just "be". We would be human "be-ings" instead of human "do-ings". We would "be" to each other, rather than "do" to each other. If we really want the world to change for the better, change has to begin within ourselves, and then the rest will fall into place.

It was during the spring/summer months of 2004 that I noticed Mel was losing strength. He tired easily, had all of a sudden developed a chronic cough, and really didn't seem to have much energy. His mood overall was pretty good. We didn't talk about it but, let me tell you, when I decided that it was time to no longer be an ostrich when it came to Mel's health, I pleaded with him to go to the doctor to find out what exactly was going on. Was it spreading to his lungs? I just about screamed the first time I saw a discarded tissue in the waste basket filled with blood. I begged him to see the doctor. That was the first and only time he fought me, not wanting to go. Well shit—do you blame him? I didn't even want him to go, but I also needed to know what was going on. Why was he so short of breath all the time?

The inner struggles you have about what to do, where to go, when to go, who to listen to, when to say yes I can do that experimental drug, yes or no to more chemotherapy, are torturous. When do you say, I am just tired of all the doctors, nurses, appointments, hospitals, clinics, needles, medication, and, eventually, oxygen tanks, and having your wife call 911 for you. When do you say enough is enough?

Cancer is like the scary monster lying in wait. You just never know when it will appear and, if it comes, will it be disguised as a lamb or a lion? Knowing that you have this death sentence hanging over your head, you have to continue to put one foot in front of the other and carry on. When I look back on the strength that both Mel and I drew from in order to get through the days ahead of us, it simply amazes me. So many times I wanted to throw my arms up towards the heavens and scream, *"Oh God, not now. We're not finished playing."* So we both put on a brave front for one another and tried to live life like we normally did, except now we were going back to the doctor for more appointments and, eventually, Mel went back on a very aggressive chemotherapy treatment. Could he handle it this time? Did he have the strength to battle the side effects?

We took a risk and planned our next winter vacation because we were convinced that this recent health scare was only a minor setback and Mel would bounce back *(... and the academy awards go to Kim and Mel Malchuk for Best Actors in a real-life nightmare).* This time, when we were deciding where we would go, normally a decision that took weeks, it took no time. We both said almost at the exact same time—Maui, Hawaii. We were not kidding ourselves any longer. We knew that this was going to be our last trip, so why not make it the most special one of all and in one of the most breathtaking places in the world—another example of what I said in an earlier chapter about how strange it was that we had this unwritten rule about not talking about the end. Yet, in both of our hearts, we knew that this vacation would be the end of our traveling as husband and wife.

Christmas of 2004 was very quiet and somber. Mel's strength was not where it should have been and his coughing and breathing only worsened. The chemo was not working and Mel really did not have the strength to continue with this aggressive treatment—not this time. Now we played the waiting game. Was the cancer back as a lamb or a lion?

It was December 30, just two days after our second year wedding anniversary and I had to rush Mel to emergency. He was having so much difficulty breathing. I was terrified, but I would not let Mel see my fear. This was the start of where our lives took a severe turn and where we both held on so tight our knuckles went completely white—just like my face did, when on a miserable cold January day, Mel's doctor said, "You guys are not going to Hawaii. Mel, we have to admit you into the hospital immediately. I'm afraid your fight has officially come to an end."

I wondered if anyone else noticed the majestic lion that just entered the room, looked me directly in the eyes, stoically sat down and was not prepared to move anytime soon. Cancer was back with an almighty roar.

Chapter Five

A Warrior Among Us

I wish I could have seen how quickly the colour drained from my face when I heard the words, "Mel, your X-rays show such an advanced spreading of cancer to not just one lung, but to almost the entire second lung. You, my man, have put up such a courageous fight against this illness that you have completely astounded me and many of my colleagues, but, Mel, you need to get your affairs in order. I'm so sorry to have to say this, but I don't ever see you leaving this hospital and going back home with Kim."

I could see the tears welling up in our doctor's eyes and hear the frog that was lodged in his throat when trying to spew those words out to us. I came to respect Mel's doctor, but not so much at first. I thought his bedside manner was ... oh, no, wait ... that was it—he didn't have a bedside manner. But over the years, I admired him for his candor and straightforwardness. He is a doctor who deals with death, and there is no room to pussyfoot around when you are dealing with such serious health issues. You want a straight shooter, someone who will not hold back just to spare your feelings. You can't afford to with this unpredictable disease.

I also knew that over the years, Mel's doctor also gained respect for Mel as his patient. Mel was strong and could take a lot. He told us many times that Mel was a medical marvel and that with the combination of medicine and positive attitude this regimen had definitely worked for us, but not any longer.

All the medical staff that came into our lives during that most horrific time were nothing less than earthly angels. To do what they do, day in and day out, with such care, grace, and honesty, they are saints. And I thanked God for them every day.

I remember Mel's doctor and nurse giving us privacy just to absorb all that we had just heard. When the door shut, I felt my knees almost start to give out and then Mel reached out for me. I am sure that if it were not for his strong arms around me, I most likely would have passed out. We just cried and held on to each other, for how long I don't know.

WOW! Holy shit! I can't catch my breath.

Even when you think you are prepared, you are never prepared to hear those words: "Get your affairs in order." We eventually broke apart and I wiped both our tears away and said to myself, *"That was your one and only time to break down in front of Mel. Don't ever do that again because he needs you to be strong, so smarten up."*

Just like that, I vowed to myself to never cry like that again in front of Mel. I could bawl my eyes out in private. He just did not need to have that on his plate right now. I would never give him reason to worry about me. He needed to see that the woman standing in front of him meant everything she said to him almost six years ago. I walked into this relationship with both eyes open and understood the consequences of that decision. I needed him to know that my word was pure, honest and true.

Mel didn't have the energy to step into the arena to slay the lion that was circling him. I would take on the role of gladiator and fight for Mel until his strength returned. I would be keeping the beast at bay until my warrior was ready to kill the predator himself. I would take care of things at home, notify family, friends and work of our situation, and I would move into the hospital that same night. Mel's hospital room would become our bachelor suite for the next while. During our stay, that room would be filled with many friends and family showing their support and love for us.

At this point, I want to focus on my family for just a bit to give you a better understanding of what they mean to me. For all the faults and mistakes my parents made when they were trying to find their footing in life, the one gift, or should I say, the seven gifts they gave to their children were that they gave us each other. If it had not been for my siblings I don't know where I would have been. I was number seven and I know, because I was told on a regular basis when growing up by my mother, that I had not been wanted. That's a pretty hard thing to digest when you are an adolescent—to hear that you were an accident, a huge mistake and that she wished she had killed you when she had the opportunity.

But something amazing happened every time my mother would spout those hurtful words to me. I always knew that I had the love of my brothers and sisters. I was the fortunate one to be the last born, because I would witness what my siblings would do that would set my mother off, which was pretty much everything.

My mother and father separated when I was only four, so my memories of my father are very few. My older siblings have filled in a lot of the missing pieces for me to know who he was but my own memories of my parents are not happy ones. I remember the terrible arguments that would break out when least expected. So at a very young age, I learned the art of walking on eggshells. I learned quickly, by watching my siblings, what not to do in order to not cause an eruption of pure hate.

Whether it's physical or emotional abuse, it really doesn't matter because it leaves scars on your spirit just the same. I will

81

fill you in on another little secret. I never blamed my mother for her actions. I only felt sorry for her. I am going to say something, that you as a reader, may find heartless, or you will be able to relate to this statement because you have felt the same way about your mother or father, or both. I did not love my mother. Just because she gave life to me, begrudgingly so, I had the choice to love her or not. I chose, at a very young age, not to love my mother because she did not earn that right, or the gift of my love.

Kiminition: on love:

People who truly love you will never hurt you, only your enemies can do that. I treated my mother as an enemy and would always be on guard with her. I am positive that if I had decided to love her, when her emotional and mental abuse came my way they would have broken me because it would have broken my heart, and that is where the deepest scars develop.

What I did feel for my mother was respect, because she earned that. I respected her for what she did for her children with only a Grade 3 education behind her. She amazed me with her resourcefulness, her hard work ethic, and I respected her for the home she always provided for me and my siblings. Okay, so it wasn't the best of circumstances, but she did the best she could with what she had and for that she has my utmost respect to this day.

My mother had a terrible upbringing as a young child. She was only two and living in the country with her siblings and grieving father when her mother died of complications giving birth to their fifth child. My grandfather re-married the wicked witch of the west, not out of love but out of necessity. He needed a caregiver for his children, so that he could continue to work in the city during the week and come back home to the country on weekends. He had to do that in order to provide for his family because there was no work for him in the country at that time. I call this "thing" that he re-married the wicked witch because she truly was a sick person. She tried to kill my mother by feeding her rat poison when she was a small child, that ended up with my mother being taken away and put in an orphanage until my grandfather could come up with plan B for his children.

Poison was not the only thing used to harm my mother and break her spirit at a very young age. She also received beatings every now and again just for the sport of it. If that wasn't bad enough, her childhood was completely robbed from her.

I am not sure what the entire circumstances were for her marrying my father or for the marriage to even be allowed in the first place; all I know is that if it were to happen in this day and age, people would be outraged. My mother was only fourteen years old when she married my father, who was twenty-five. What does a fourteen-year-old girl know about being a wife? Absolutely nothing, but those were different times—a time that I am so grateful not to have been a part of. Women did not have a voice in the thirties and were forced to grow up very quickly. Life was hard and not filled with a lot of joy back then. You did what you had to do to survive in hopes of possibly making a better life for yourself and for your children.

How could I possibly blame my mother for not showing me love? I don't think my mother had a hot clue how to love another person, because I know she most likely never experienced what it was like to be loved. Not only did she not love herself, I have a sneaking suspicion that she barely liked herself. I would sometimes catch glimpses of the lighter side of my mother when growing up and only wished she could stay in that light because I know she would have had a much happier life.

By the time I was a young adult and no longer living at home, I had learned to forgive my mother for her treatment of me. It was the only way for me to build as normal a life as I could for myself. When my visits with my mother would come to an end during that time, I would hug her and make a point of telling her that I loved her. I remember the look on her face the first time she heard those words come from my mouth to her ears. It was as though I had spoken in a foreign tongue. She was stunned and I got the very sad impression that she had not heard those words directed to her for a very long time. I could see her inner pain when looking into her eyes. It was almost as though she had to force or choke the words out that she loved me too.

I remember driving home after one of our visits crying to myself, thinking of how tortured my mother's life had been. Her past constantly haunted her and she used her pain and anger as a crutch until the day she died.

My mother chose to live out her days as a victim, another perfect example of what can happen to your life if the past is always invading the present. You are never able to move forward and have the life that you want. I am thankful to my mother for showing me how **not** to live life. I only wish she knew that she truly did teach me something of great value. She taught me how to not ever be a victim in life and that lesson would come back to me when I realized I was playing that exact role in my first marriage.

I believe that we can break the cycle of abuse if we want to or we can play the victim because of it, and make everyone who comes into our life pay for the way we were raised. I know that I broke the cycle because people who come into my life are amazed when they hear stories of my childhood. They cannot believe that I am filled with so much love, considering I was never shown any when growing up. I tell them that I might not have received it from my mother, but I was surrounded by it from my siblings. If it were not for the love of my siblings, I know I would not be where I am today. They took the brunt of my mother's rage and, by the time I came into the world, she was too exhausted and really had no interest in mothering me. I am thankful for that gift and consider myself the fortunate one to have missed the majority of her rages and her lack of "mothering skills".

Don't get me wrong, she was a fighter right up until the end of her life, but I always stood up to her when she tried to make me feel small and worthless. I would not let her make me a victim like she was. Had it not been for the constant love, laughter and protection my siblings provided me, I would not have had the courage to stand up to her when I needed to shield my spirit, which she so often tried to break.

I am sure that one reason Mel married me was so that he could get my sisters as his sisters-in-law. He loved them. He could not believe how much we loved each other as a family and was thrilled that he could be a small part of it. He said that our laughter and love was intoxicating, and who could help wanting to spend time with my loving and crazy family. I knew that my family was very special and just the exact medicine that Mel needed. When all my sisters flew in from out of town and walked into Mel's hospital room wearing their Ya-Ya Sisterhood Headdresses chanting "Ya-Ya"—I thought Mel was going to, pardon the pun, die right there and then. If he didn't know it before, it was confirmed right at that moment that he was officially their brother-in-law and he was loved by all of them. If I had not kept my sense of humour throughout that whole ordeal and every day since then, I am sure I would not be where I am today in my recovery. I am not even sure I would "be" had I not kept my humour at the forefront. Laughter is so healthy, and a great release of stress. Mel appreciated the love and especially the laughter that was flowing out of everyone who came to see him.

The outpouring of sentiments and tenderness from family and friends was amazing during this time. It was incredible and Mel was so grateful to all who came to see him. Love and laughter are the two most important qualities of life, especially at a time like that.

The call that I dreaded to make was the one to the funeral home, but we were being a responsible and mature couple doing what needed to be done. We made arrangements to meet with the funeral director so that Mel could make his final plans. Rick, the director, would end up being another one of my earthly angels. The minute we met, we all felt comfortable with each other. Well, as much as anyone can feel comfortable arranging their own funeral service.

My God, Mel handled himself with such dignity and control; he was simply amazing to watch. The strength and courage he showed me countless times made me so proud to be his wife. Rick could see that we were not ready for what was happening. We were both young with still so much life to live, so in love and not nearly ready to give up the fight, but we needed to get things arranged.

We knew that we were not at all interested in a morbid, religious service. Instead we wanted it to be a celebration of Mel's life. We wanted the service to be tasteful, memorable, light-hearted and, most importantly, conducted by someone who would reflect on the spiritual side of life. We wanted something inspirational rather than religious.

Rick, of course, had the perfect man in mind for us and we arranged to meet with this gentleman later on in the week. I had not realized how draining the meeting would be for both of us and I remember Mel fell asleep early that night. Perhaps a lot of pressure was taken off him, knowing that arrangements were underway. I know he took care of it more for me than for himself, so that I would not be heavily burdened with trying to figure out what he would have wanted at a time when I probably would not be able to formulate a sentence.

Mel was sleeping peacefully whereas I, on the other hand, was wide awake. My thoughts of the day would not allow me to fall asleep. The chair/cot that had become my bed for the last week was positioned right in front the window. I opened the curtain just a wee bit to let the lights from outside come in but, hopefully, not disturb Mel. Earlier that same day, I had bought my first journal, just for this situation. I knew that I was not going to be able to sleep another night. I had so many things running through my head, so many fears, so many things that I

wanted to say, but there was no way I was going to burden Mel
with any of my concerns. I already knew that he was worried
about leaving me behind, because he told me that on a few different occasions. Yet, I needed to get my thoughts out or I would
start going crazy.

This was the start of my journaling and I thank God every
day for having started the ritual. My journal became my safety
net, confidant, friend, therapist and salvation at a time when I
needed to occupy my mind. The choice to start journaling was
the smartest and healthiest thing I did for myself, and for Mel,
during a time of total fear, solitude and hopelessness. I am only
speaking for myself when I say this, but I did not want to burden my friends and family with my worries, yet I needed a
means of expression to get my thoughts out. I could not, especially at the time of Mel's hospitalization, keep everything bottled up inside of me, because I am sure I would have started to
unravel in front everyone, including Mel. I was not going to
allow that to happen. I was being strong for Mel and my fear
was that if I chose to tell loved ones around me how frightened
I was at the thought of continuing a life without my husband,
they might have told Mel, and then he would focus on me
rather than on his health.

So I would not unload my uncertainties on anyone, but use
my journals as an instrument to get me through the unknown. I
credit my journals for getting me through a lot of lonely and
empty nights over the past two years. Were it not for them, I
know that I would not be where I am today.

A few more days and nights had passed since I started writing my thoughts into my journal and I was feeling lighter
because of it. I was also bringing in a "special tea" concoction
called Essiac that had been recommended to me by one of my
sisters. Mel was not a believer in alternative medicines, but at
that stage he was willing to try anything. Then, a miracle happened. Mel's doctor, Dr. Crawford *(who was another one of our*

angels), came into our room holding Mel's latest set of X-rays. I could tell by his body language that he was there to give us good news—not bad. Dr. Crawford had a smile on his face as he said, "Okay Mel, things are actually looking better, so whatever we are doing, let's keep doing it. We will take another set of X-rays in a couple of days, and, if they look as clear as this set, or better, you might be able to get out of here."

Well, my jaw almost hit the ground. Had I just heard right? Go home? Was I sending out a much better message to the universe because of my thoughts and state of mind from my journal entries? Was the tea having a positive effect on Mel's system? Did all the love and laughter that Mel received over the past ten days from family and friends make a difference? Yes! Yes! And yes! Another gift had been handed to us. With love, laughter, and positive thoughts going out to the universe, you can achieve anything you want. Our thoughts really do control the outcomes in our lives.

We were home again and it felt like heaven to be able to sleep in the same bed, to enjoy meals together, to lie on the couch and cuddle, to watch some discovery show on the deadliest snakes in the world—who cared what we were watching. A miracle was just given to us in the form of time. All that mattered was that my husband was home with me and I was lying in his arms again. I was so thankful for this turn of events because it finally answered the nagging question I had carried around for so many years. I wanted to know and get an actual sign that if I truly and unselfishly asked the universe for help, would I receive my gifts? Would HP answer my prayers? Or, would HP ignore me because I don't go to church every Sunday? Well, let's see. Mel, after being told to make his funeral arrangements because he had to get his affairs in order, was now back at home with me after being released from the hospital. You be the judge.

This lesson taught me once and for all that if you believe and send out positive thoughts to the universe and not focus on the negative, you, too, will soon be living in a magical life.

The remainder of January went by, February, and then almost all of March, until I had to call 911 for the last time. Mel was just not getting enough oxygen into his lungs. I knew even before seeing the last set of X-rays in the emergency room that he was not coming home with me ever again. Mel had played all his miracle cards in this final game of life. He was so congested, and his oxygen intake needed to be much higher than we could give him at home. They also needed to start managing his anxiety with medication, so home care was not an option any longer. It was at this point, that I didn't want Mel to be at home either. I was scared and ill equipped to handle the stage that he was now in. I wanted the best care for him and knew that there was only one place where he could get that. The medical staff was trained, capable and so caring I couldn't help admiring the way they not only looked after Mel, but were also wonderful with me.

It was during that last stay at the hospital that I would meet my final angel. Linda was the social worker for Cancer Care. She would come by and talk with Mel or me, or both of us. It was strange. Linda would just magically show up when we needed to talk to her and then just disappear when we wanted to be alone. It wasn't strange at all. It was the universe working its magic again.

I would end up leaning on Linda in the months ahead. I had no idea the depth of pain that I was going to be facing during my grieving period—not a clue.

I lived in Mel's hospital room for just a little over four weeks. I could see his health deteriorating as the weeks went by. He could be very difficult at times and my heart went out to the particular staff member who happened to be on his hit list that day. He was going through the anger portion of dealing with death. He wasn't ready. He was not ready to let me go and I knew that. It got to the point where he just refused to sleep. When I talked to him about it and finally got it out of him, he said that he was afraid to go to sleep for fear that he would never get up again and that just couldn't happen because he still had so much to do. So he just fought it and, my God, he literally fought it to the bitter end.

Mel was taking so much medication and his oxygen level was so high, that his thought process was really jumbled at times. That was really upsetting for me near the end. He was not acting like my Mel. He was becoming a stranger to me and disappearing right before my eyes. Yet there were times in the day when I would get glimpses of the man who literally "rocked my world" the first time he kissed me. I will never forget how powerful that kiss was. It is memories like those that make you stay and put up with or simply ignore the mood swings, because you promised to love this person for better or for worse. Even at his worst, I could not love him any less or more than I did.

It occurred to me during the final days that I was a big part of the problem. I thought that my staying at the hospital was the thing I was supposed to do. I was supposed to be there for him, by his side no matter what. I was his wife and promised to look after him in sickness and in health. If he were to have a breathing spasm during the night, I was the one who would be there to pound on his back, to check that his oxygen levels were high enough, to ensure his tube was not kinked or blocked somehow.

But things were not good that last week. I was frustrated because he was being so ornery and there was just no reasoning with him. He was upsetting the staff, not taking his medication, not following rules, smoking every once in awhile *(don't judge)* and he was basically ignoring me and mad at me because, well, just because.

I finally made the decision that it was time for me to go home. I talked to Dr. Crawford and told him of my revelation, but I wanted his opinion first. Was that the right thing to do or would it just make him more agitated? I just didn't know what to do anymore and I needed his advice. I told him I thought I was making it worse by staying and knew that Mel was only hanging on for me. I knew this because I had woken up in the middle of the night to see him sitting up staring at me. I asked him once, "What are you doing up, baby. Why are you not sleeping?" He replied, "I'm watching an angel sleep." I could see how tired he was and I was so exhausted myself, I felt like a walking zombie and the lack of sleep was contributing to my frustration.

I am not sure how many hours Mel slept his last week, but I can tell you that it was probably not even half of what a normal, healthy person would have had in that same period. The amount of medication they were giving him to sleep should have knocked out an elephant, but not my Mel. He was fighting it. He was fighting for me.

When I told Dr. Crawford that I would be packing up and leaving, he said that he thought that would be a good idea and that the staff was actually thinking about suggesting that to me for Mel's sake. I went back into Mel's room and started to pack. I could hear the worry in Mel's voice when he asked what was going on, why was I leaving? (God that was so hard it just about killed me.) I simply told him that my back was sore from sleeping on the cot and that I thought maybe sleeping in our own bed for a few nights would help me out. I assured him that I would be back tomorrow and that he could call me from his room anytime, and if he wanted me to come back I would. He seemed okay with that explanation.

My sister, Rose, flew in from out of town to spend time with us. When I finally got home from leaving the hospital, with bag in hand, I just didn't want to talk about anything. It was just so hard to leave him there by himself, alone with his own thoughts. But the more I thought about it, the more I knew it was what he needed. Maybe he wanted to break down, to pray, to be angry, to simply "be" with it, and stop being strong on my account.

It became obvious to me within the next couple of hours that I had made the right choice to leave the hospital and come home in order to give him some alone time. I knew that because he called throughout the evening just to talk, wanting to know what we were up to, and his sense of humour was back. In these brief conversations, Mel sounded like his old self again and he seemed to be in a much a better place. How frightened he must have been near the end, but he never complained about anything. He never said how unfair life was. He never got angry at God. He accepted the hand that was dealt to him. I never once heard him say that he felt sorry for himself.

After the calls stopped and I was about to get myself into bed, I decided to phone the nurse's station to see how he was doing. They said that he had finally laid down and looked as though he would be out for the night, for me not to worry, and to finally get some sleep myself. If anything changed they would call me, but for now he was sleeping peacefully. That's all I needed to hear. He was in the best care and that's all I could have hoped for.

I phoned the hospital the next morning and they didn't want to alarm me but they needed me to get down as soon as I could, as they were having a small problem with Mel. He was packing all his clothes and he wanted them to call a taxi to pick him up and take him home because he wanted to surprise me. That would have been one hell of a surprise, to see Mel walk through our door at home. I drove like a maniac back to the hospital and when I got there, I saw Mel sitting in a wheelchair with his oxygen tank, his jacket and shoes on and his suitcase packed. Well sort of—but he wanted me to get the message—he wanted to get the hell out of there and go home.

Oh God, how am I going to tell him no? It will just break his heart to tell him that he has to stay here and that the next home he is going to is in a totally different dimension. When I reached him sitting in the wheelchair, I bent down to look into his face and he simply said, "Hi Poochkin. How are you?" I just kind of shook my head, chuckled, and said "great" and how about we get back to our room. No problem at all. I was thankful for that small miracle. I just did not want to see him upset anymore.

The radio was set to our favourite light jazz station. I remember the room being so toasty warm that afternoon, a contrast to the miserable day outside that matched my mood. We had some lunch and then I got him to take his shoes and jacket off. We talked about the *"Great Escape"* he had planned earlier that morning and he agreed with me that the hospital was the best place for him right now. Then he did something very surprising. He asked me to call the head nurse and Dr. Crawford into his room. When they both came in, we were all a little unsure what to expect. Mel apologized to them and asked if they would please pass on his apologies to any other staff member whom he might have offended or hurt. He said that that was never his intention, he just wanted to go home and feel like a human being again. He said that so much of his independence had been stripped away from him that he didn't even feel like a man any longer and that, unfortunately, he was just lashing out at whoever was close by. They reassured him that their staff was used to things that are much worse than a little tongue lashing, but they thanked him for his consideration nonetheless and, as they left our room, said they would definitely let other staff members know.

Apologizing was not one of Mel's strongest attributes so, when he did, my heart broke into a million pieces because I knew how difficult it had been for him in the past, but not so much this time. The words just flowed so easily out of him. I saw a change in him, so at peace, not caring about image or persona any longer. Apologize because it's the right thing to do; it is definitely not a sign of weakness but one of strength.

We were having a quiet moment and just staring at each other for awhile when a song came on the radio and he asked me if I would like the next dance. Well, of course I jumped at the opportunity to dance with my husband. Could that man dance? I just fit right into his arms and we started to slow dance. Tears were rolling down my face and getting his T-shirt soaked because I knew I would never dance with my husband ever again. He grabbed my face and I saw that he was crying too because he knew it as well. I asked him if there was anything he wanted me to run out and get for him, did he need anything. He just looked at me and said, "I would really like to make love to you one last time."

Well, that was it. I walked over to the bed, turned down the blankets, closed the drapes and we both crawled into bed. This was the most intimate we had been with each other since his being admitted into the hospital for the last time. Our love making had pretty much come to an end in the previous six months, but there was something much more erotic that took its place. We would sometimes just sit and stare at each other or simply hold hands for hours and not say a word because our eyes were telling each other everything we simply could not put into words. There is something far more intimate about that kind of love making. So, to be lying in his arms again was almost orgasmic. We both fell asleep in a matter of minutes and there was just absolutely no place I wanted to be but right there in the nook of his arm. I eventually got up, carefully, so I would not wake him but, of course, he stirred and asked where I was going. I told him that I would be at home if he needed me, but if he wanted me to stay I would. He was so wonderful and he said that he would be okay and that he promised he would not make a run for the door again.

I wanted to take advantage of this time because Mel seemed so lucid. God had given him back to me for these few hours. I went to the bedside and was running my fingers through his beautiful, curly salt-and-pepper hair. I said that I had something really important to tell him and I needed his full attention. I told him that I was so proud to be his wife and that I had no regrets. If I had to do it all over again, I would do it exactly the same, and then I said, *"If you want to hang on for yourself then do so, but if you are fighting to stay for me, you don't have to fight anymore. If there is anything that this situation has done for me, or that I have learned from just watching you over the last month, it is how to be strong. You know my family and friends. I will not be alone. They will never let that happen. I will be okay. You have made sure of that."*

I remember that his reply upset me at the time, but later on, I would recall his words and smile to myself. He said, *"I don't want you to pass on love should it ever come your way again. Please don't be a martyr. I know that you will pick wisely, but, Kim, if you decide to go through the rest of your life alone because of your love for me, that would be wrong. You have so much love inside of you to give, it would be a waste to not share that gift with someone deserving of it. You deserve to be loved and I want someone to be there for you. I hate knowing that you are going to be alone for awhile and that's why it's been hard for me to let go, but I am so tired, Kim. I just wanted you to know that I would be okay with you loving again."*

I knew what he was trying to tell me, but I just could not hear it at that moment because my world was coming to a crashing halt. We told each other we loved one another and that we would see each other tomorrow. We kissed goodbye and that was the end to our perfect Saturday afternoon—an afternoon filled with many little miracles for me to treasure, an afternoon I will never forget.

I came home completely drained. I told Rose about how I was sure that I had just received a gift from the universe. HP gave Mel back to me and it was so good to see him again. How I had missed him and I was grateful to have my husband back if only for a few hours.

During that night as I was lying in our bed at home, there was a stillness that was so unnerving. I felt, in the pit of my stomach, that my life was about to take a drastic detour. No phone calls were coming from Mel's room at the hospital and I had this empty feeling that I could not shake.

I fell asleep reflecting on our beautiful afternoon and then the next thing I remember was the phone ringing at 8:20 a.m. The hospital was asking me to get down as quickly as I could, as they could see the end for Mel was very near. I made the call to Mel's son, Maury, to get to the hospital and said that I would meet him there. The weather was awful, the wind was cold and the sky was grey—very appropriate for the feeling of the day in general.

Rose drove me to the hospital because I was not even going to attempt to make that drive. When we arrived, Maury and Audrey, Mel's daughter-in-law, were already by his side. The four of us huddled around Mel, talked softly and quietly, rubbed his feet and hands as I just stared at him, watching him sleep. He looked so peaceful, so beautiful—my warrior. His breathing pattern changed. He gasped once, then regular breathing resumed, but not for very long. With a deafening roar that was meant for only me to hear, the door opened, the lion stood up, and slowly walked out of the room—in search of his next warrior.

Chapter Six

A State of Numb

I now understand what happened to me, as Mel took his last breath, but I did not comprehend it then.

Where are my tears? Why am I not screaming at the top of my lungs? Why am I not completely losing my mind at this very moment? My world has just changed in this very instant and I am not falling apart at the seams.

I was convinced, as I was standing by my husband's deathbed, that as his soul left his body it snatched my heart along with it. That had to be the explanation for why I felt nothing. There was this huge void in my chest where my heart used to be. That was why I couldn't feel. No heart—no feeling, right?

Well, I won't keep you in suspense. The human body and all its intricate parts is an absolutely amazingly crafted masterpiece. The brain immediately took over at that moment.

Kiminition: on my inner state:

My brain was assembling a meeting with the rest of my body parts and it went something like this. "Okay organs, let's gather around. Well, this is the moment that we have all been dreading, but have also been training really hard for. Okay, first up, arms and legs. *Your job is pretty much the same. Just keep moving. It's okay if sometimes you actually look like a robot. People will understand that she is trying to find her footing again. The most important thing is that you have to carry her weight, and she is carrying a pretty heavy load right now, so your job is to make sure she doesn't fall.*

Next—stomach. Yeah, you won't be seeing much food for at least a year so get over it and don't complain.

Okay, where are the eyes? I want the eyes up front because they have a few things to do. You two have to stay clear so that when she is out in public she doesn't hurt herself or someone else because she can't see through her tears. But in the privacy of her own home, do your stuff and let the tears flow. Tears are not a sign of weakness. They're a sign of healing. The most important thing you two need to do is ensure that you are ready for her to see the signs that she will be sent every now and again, to let her know that someone is watching out for her.

Okay, we are almost finished, so now where are the lungs? Okay you guys, you two are going to get inundated with tar and nicotine, but the good news is that it won't last long, so be patient.

Last but not least, where is our heart? Well my friend, you have definitely taken a beating and that is why I am here to help you out. The only thing I ask of you now is that you just keep on pumping.

I will look after the feeling part because that's my job. I will protect Kim's heart by putting layers of protection around it so that she will feel only what I think she needs to feel at any given time. As time goes on, I will slowly remove each one of those layers so that she can start the healing process, because in order to heal, she has to be able to feel. Okay troops—she is counting on us. Let's do her proud. This meeting is over."

When I talked to Linda, my social worker from the hospital, I asked her why it was that when I felt I was making progress, all of sudden I could be pulled quickly backwards and feel I was at square one all over again. What was going on? I felt like a yo-yo with my emotions. She called it back sliding and, simply put, she explained that my brain is and has been protecting my heart from the moment Mel passed. As humans, we cannot take in or even begin to comprehend the pain and the meaning of death all at once, especially when it hits so close to home. The brain is an amazing organ. It knew that it had to kick in because, if it didn't, the pain and hurt I was feeling were so extreme and traumatic that my heart might not have been able to sustain it and simply have given out. Think about that.

We have all heard stories of how sometimes when people get the terrible news that someone they love has been taken away from them far too soon, they end up dying themselves of a heart attack, or they go into a deep depression and can't ever seem to turn it around. So I ask you this question. Do you think someone could actually die from a broken heart?

When I walked out of Mel's room, the medical staff that was on duty that afternoon was absolutely amazing. Their heartfelt condolences touched me to the core. The kind words they said to me about how much the staff talked about us as a couple made me realize again how blessed I was to have experienced this kind of love in my lifetime. The nurses were envious of the love we shared, but, most importantly, Mel knew that he was deeply and truly loved.

They also thought that it was important for me to know how much he talked about me when I wasn't around. He was so proud to be my husband. He knew I had changed his life for the better. Mel was convinced that if I hadn't come into his life he would not have seen his only grandchild born, and he would not have found true love. How could he be angry at God for giving him so many treasures before taking him back home? I don't think you can ever give a greater gift to anyone as they are preparing to leave this world than telling them truly and lovingly that their life mattered. I knew that I could not love a person more than I loved Mel and, what was even better, was hearing those reassuring words from his medical staff and knowing that he knew it too.

I remember waiting for one of Mel's cousins, Ron, who was like a brother to him, to arrive at the hospital. I could not sit and wait any longer. I wanted to leave the place that had become my second home over the last few months and run home, curl up and die. Well, wouldn't you know it? When I finally got home, Ron was at the hospital. My girlfriend, Hayley, *(my eternal sister)* had been waiting for me at home and offered to drive me back to the hospital.

The subsequent conversation I had with Ron was really not of any great importance. We hugged, consoled each other, and talked about the next few days ahead of us. But something heavenly happened to me when I was leaving the hospital for the second time that day. There was a reason why I was meant to go back. The weather was still miserable and so it should have been. I noticed when I walked out of the hospital doors that everyone around me was acting like nothing had changed. Life was carrying on. People were complaining about the miserable weather. They were walking around, driving their cars, talking to friends. I just felt like screaming, *"What is going on? What is wrong with all of you people? The world has just lost an amazing man."*

I wanted people to know that the world as they knew it would never be the same. If my world had changed, then, damn it, I wanted everybody else's world to change too. I didn't want to be alone in this agony. A poem by W. H. Auden comes to mind that so eloquently says how I was feeling when I walked through those hospital doors for the very last time. It is called Funeral Blues.

Stop all the clocks, cut off the telephones
Prevent the dogs from barking with a juicy bone

A State of Numb

Silence the pianos with muffled drum
Bring out the coffin, let the mourners come

Let airplanes circle moaning overhead
Scribbling in the sky, the message, he is dead
Put crepe bows round the necks of the public doves
Let the traffic policemen wear black cotton gloves

He was my North, my South, my East and my West
My working week, and my Sunday rest
My noon, my midnight, my talk, my song
I thought love would last forever, I was wrong

The stars are not wanted, put out every one
Pack up the moon and dismantle the sun
Pour away the oceans and sweep up the woods
For nothing now can ever come to any good.

The wind was howling and it felt as if it were blowing right through me. As I was waiting for traffic to pass to get back into the car with Hayley, I thought I heard my name being called. I ignored it, thinking it was the wind or my mind playing tricks on me. Who would be calling me back anyway? Did Ron have something else to say to me? Then I heard it again—clear as can be—*Kim!* I turned back to see who wanted my attention.

No one was there, only a lone seagull, flying just above my head away from the hospital. I stood there in amazement. I knew it was a sign that Mel's spirit and soul were free at last. Free from all his pains and worries.

I am thankful to this day for that enormous gift the universe chose to give me when I needed it most. It was almost like HP reached down and put its arm around my shoulders and said, *"Don't worry about him, Kim. He will never be alone. He passed all the tests that he was meant to learn in this lifetime.*

There are no more lessons for him to learn on Earth, so now it's time for him to come back home."

This was a critical lesson for me to learn and to share with others. Mel was never mine to keep. We are not property. We are gifts given to each other for an undetermined amount of time. Unless you are clairvoyant and can predict the future, love like it's your last day, so that you have no regrets if you have no tomorrow.

I am so grateful to my brain for rallying all the troops to get me through making the final arrangements for Mel's Celebration of Life. Looking back on it today, had my brain not kicked in and put this invisible shield around my heart, I would not have gotten through the next few days. I remember being almost robotic and just wanting to keep my mind busy so that I would not have to think about anything else, just the task at hand. That's all I could do—just one thing at a time.

The days that followed, right up to the day of the service, were so gloomy, cold and depressing—and then came the day to pay tribute to my husband.

The sun was shining and there was hardly any breeze. We could not have wanted a better day. The chapel was filled to capacity with family, friends, co-workers, baseball players, and even some of Mel's medical staff.

I wanted to say something to my guests about the man who changed my life, but I wondered if I could. Could I get up in front of everyone and tell them all how incredible this man was without completely making a blubbering fool of myself? I was trying to find a poem in books or on the Internet that I could read that would convey the power of our love. My search was fruitless, so then I thought, why don't I try to write something? I knew what I wanted to say, so I sat in front of the computer and it was like a miracle. It seemed like the words were typing out themselves. It was the strangest feeling, yet very comforting for me, and then, after maybe less than thirty minutes, I had my poem:

A State of Numb

I am missing you so much already
But I know that I need to stand tall and steady
The years that we have spent
Oh, what they have meant

It was an honor to stand by your side
What a wonderful life we shared, what a wonderful ride
Everyday I would rush home to you
Because I knew that what we shared was true

You were so brave and so strong
How could our love be wrong
You kept me from all sorts of harms
In the comfort and safety in your arms

You were larger than life
And I was so proud to be your wife
We were so lucky and so blessed
We really did have it among all the rest

I write these words for all to hear
So they know that you were cherished and so very dear
I know that I will always long for your embrace
And will miss seeing your beautiful face

But all that I will have to do
Is close my eyes just to see you
You are part of my heart and soul
And for that you made me whole

I will always have a piece of you and I know that sounds silly
But how can anyone deny that, you are a part of Gilly
You were truly God's gift to me
And now I must find the strength to set you free

You will forever be in my heart
But I knew that right from the very start
I know that one day, and it just has to be
You and I will be together again for all eternity

I was able to read the words in front of everyone while keeping my composure and dignity intact. I did not realize it at the time but the only reason I was able to get through it was because I was completely numb. I was in a daze and just going through the motions of life.

One of Mel's requests was to have a video tribute. It was set to music that we both loved and the pictures that I picked captured the life and the loves of what made Mel, Mel.

After the service, one of Mel's cousins had a get-together back at her home. It was wonderful to be surrounded by Mel's family but, to be honest with you, I was emotionally and physically exhausted. I just wanted to go home and be with my own family, put on my pajamas and sit in peace.

We had a very quiet night at home, no phone calls, no flowers being delivered, no one dropping off food, nothing, complete silence, and I welcomed it. It was exactly what I needed. To be with the people who loved me, who loved Mel, and who could make me laugh—if I could muster up the energy to do so. I remember opening up all the cards our guests had picked out for me as a source of comfort and, let me tell you, all of them and their messages of love, strength and encouragement were like having a warm blanket wrapped around me. Of course, my sisters, who are pillars of strength, read the heartfelt messages and wept right along side me. The most amazing thing was that there were over 100 cards and only one duplicate. They were all unique and contained their own private and different messages. I couldn't believe that, and it still remains with me today. For those of you who don't think cards matter or make a difference, I'm telling you they really do.

Then the day arrived when my family was going to leave. I would truly be alone. I was so scared of that day coming, yet I knew I needed to stand on my own two feet and just persevere. The minute they left, I ran to get the DVD from Mel's tribute. I slid it into the player and must have watched it at least a dozen times, crying harder each time it played. This was the first day that I just completely broke down. It was the first time that I was left on my own and I really wanted to let go and, just for once, not be strong for anyone. I had not wanted my family and friends to worry about me, so I had put on a brave front, something that I was used to doing, but, now that everyone was gone, I just needed to let go and feel what I needed to feel by myself.

I mentioned earlier what my saving grace was during this very difficult and unstable time of my life. The choice to journal my thoughts, experiences, fears, and longings was the best choice I ever made for myself. Still, to this day I fill the pages with my thoughts. I have made a point every day since Mel passed of writing to him in my journals. I really feel as though he is still listening intently to what I am saying.

That was one of the things that I believe really made our relationship work. We communicated with one another. We valued each other's take on things and always respected what the other had to say. I knew not having that was going to be one of the greatest voids in my life going forward. Not being able to ask Mel for his opinion on this or that was going to be a huge adjustment.

But in my journals I could, and people wouldn't have to know that I was finding comfort in sharing my thoughts and worries with the ghost of my husband. My journal became my best friend, just like my cigarettes did. I know those of you who don't smoke simply cannot understand how anyone could love smoking. But those of you who do smoke totally understand what I'm talking about. My cigarettes and journals were always there for me.

The nights were the worst. Oh, who am I kidding? Every waking hour shortly after Mel's passing was awful. All I knew was that I needed to do something to occupy my mind or I would have driven myself crazy. That was when, no matter what time of day or night, I turned to my journals. I could escape my reality and get lost for hours.

Journals are for you and you alone. They are private and for your eyes only. Should you want to share your writings with someone else, that is your choice. I chose not to share my words with anyone. In your journals, you can say anything you are thinking and feeling without having to justify those thoughts to anyone. My journals afforded me the opportunity to write about every emotion I was feeling. You name the emotion, and, I probably wrote about it. It felt safe to get everything out that was weighing so heavily on my mind.

I wrote approximately 500 pages during that time, and, when I read over my entries, I saw there was a common theme. I was thankful and grateful for the life that I shared with Mel. I celebrated what we had as opposed to what we had lost. But now here comes the real shocker: I wrote, over and over again, how I would not have changed one single thing about our life, not even Mel's cancer.

Kiminition: on the role that cancer played in our lives:

I want to continue explaining my views on the eternal world. Not that I am trying to convince you of anything, because I am not. I am just sharing what I believe to be true because it gets me through.

Remember when I said that we all decided when, who and how we were going to experience earthly life? It's like we signed a contract and agreed to the terms within that contract. Our earthly life was mapped out for us. In those terms that we agreed to, we also chose how we were going to leave Earth.

Mel decided that his fate would be cancer and here is why I think that. Mel decided to come to Earth and be part of the 50s. That was an era of many exciting times, but it was also a time that men were raised, much like today but perhaps not to the same degree, to not show their emotions, to not talk about their feelings or admit that they made a mistake, because that would show weakness.

Well, all of that thinking was going to be thrown out with the garbage once he received the news that he was dying. When you get news like that, you look at what is really important in life and start getting your priorities in order. This ending gave Mel an opportunity to, perhaps, heal past relationships that he would never have had if he had not been diagnosed with cancer. Cancer actually made Mel grow as a person. It made him softer, sweeter, and more sincere. It made him appreciate family and friends much more. It made him love deeper—so obvious to anyone seeing him with his granddaughter, Gillian.

Grandparenthood gave Mel the chance to be a better parent the second time around. It was almost like cancer made Mel do everything better when given a second opportunity. He was an incredible partner, in that he was very giving, caring and gentle.

I met Mel when I was supposed to meet him, because I am telling you right now, if I had met the Mel that he was twenty years prior (and I am sure his ex-wife would not disagree with me) I most likely would have hated that cocky, arrogant and stubborn man. No, I got him when I was supposed to get him and that meant cancer and all.

That is my take on how cancer really enriched our relationship. It made us focus on what was important. We just simply did not have time to bicker about small issues. Hey, don't get me wrong, our relationship wasn't always picture perfect. We fought. But, thankfully, not often.

You definitely need that friction from time to time to create a little passion, but in our case, we could not lose sight of the fact that we just did not have time on our side for petty arguments. The other thing that cancer forced us to do was to say what we wanted to say to each other because we didn't know what the next day was going to spring on us. My heart goes out to anyone who has lost the love of their life without having had the opportunity to tell them one last time how much they were loved.

A really good example of this was the day that the Twin Towers in New York came under siege. I know that almost everyone remembers exactly what they were doing when they first heard the horrific news. I got to work that dreadful morning and everyone was glued to the TV set in one of our conference rooms. I remember running to my desk, knowing that Mel was still sleeping, but I just had to wake him up to tell him what had just occurred.

As the day progressed, the news got worse and people were literally walking around in a haze. How could this be happening? Why is this happening?

I remember breaking down a few times that day, thinking of all the husbands and wives, young and old, who would never see each other ever again ... simply because they had gone to work that day. How incredibly unfair that is. But I also hoped secretly to myself that everyone saw the hidden life lesson that the universe wants us to learn so desperately from that horrible historic event—slow down and get your priorities in order! Tell the people in your life who matter to you that you love them every time you leave them and when you are with them. You just never know when your time is up and the universe will want you back home. I make a point whenever I get the chance of telling friends and family that I love them.

When I got home that evening, even before I said anything, Mel said to me, "We are so lucky that we know how important it is to tell each other that we love one another every day, because who knows what will happen."

I just smiled because I knew that we both got the message loud and clear and had been living that lesson long before 9/11 had occurred. How blessed were we to have already figured that one out all by ourselves? I guess you can say that Mel's cancer was our own personal 9/11 experience, which we were living on a daily basis.

Linda would call me from time to time to check in on me and see how I was doing. I remember telling her during one of those phone conversations about how upset I was that I was not dreaming about Mel. I missed him so much and was asking the universe to bring him back to me in my dreams. Why was this not happening? I wasn't being completely ridiculous and asking to bring him back to me in real life. If that were the case, it would require someone calling the crazy-mobile and have them strap a white jacket on me and take me away. I was simply asking to see and talk to him in my dreams. So what gives?

She told me the most comforting thing, which I will never forget. Linda said that the reason why Mel was not coming to me in my dreams was because we said all that we needed to say to one another in this lifetime. When people dream of their loved ones who have passed, it's usually because they have unfinished business with them. They still had something that they wanted to say to that person but were either too afraid to say it to them, or just never got around to it. When she told me that, I knew she was right, but I had to be reminded of that fact.

Cancer made us not waste time or opportunities because we didn't know if we had a tomorrow. If there is one message I want you to take away from my story it's that you should take the opportunity to tell the people who really matter how much they mean to you, especially your life partner. The gifts that you will get in return will astound you.

Chapter Seven

Table for One

What do you do when you still feel like you are part of a couple and then realize that your partner is no longer there? Your partner is never going to be sitting across from you at the dinner table ever again, so why are you setting the table for two?

You pick up the phone to call home because you want to ask your partner a question and then you remember in mid-stride, oh yeah, no one will answer the phone because they are not at home.

You come home from grocery shopping and just realize that you have bought enough food for two, but the funniest thing is that you can't even remember the last time you actually ate something.

I could go on and give you more examples of situations that a survivor finds themselves in because of conditioning or habit. But once we stop and take a look at what we are doing or what we were about to do, it makes us feel that we are slowly losing our minds.

Before I continue on with my story, you are going to get another Kiminition on the label "widow":

I will never refer to myself as a widow. I hate that word. Who in their right mind came up with that one? Even before I became that statistical checkbox on forms, I had despised that word. Instantly you feel sorry for whoever fits into that category.

I associate the word "widow" with the black widow spider. Now, everything that I have seen or read about these femme fatale venomous spiders is that they kill and eat their male friends after mating. So when I have a form in front of me and I come to the marital status section, by checking off "widow" I am basically saying that I'm a murderess.

Can you see logic behind this reasoning? It's all about word association for me.

I say we abolish the words "widow" and "widower" from all forms, dictionaries, oh hell, from the English language altogether, and replace it with something more appropriate, like "survivor". It's genderless, accurate and much more dignified.

The first time I had to fill out a form after the loss of Mel, when I came to that section tears came to my eyes and I started feeling sorry for myself. It's just not right that a form should make you feel that way. That label has such a negative and isolating connotation to it.

Case in point: Tell someone you are a widow and instantly you see their facial expression change right before your eyes. It's like you have just told them that you have a fatal disease, but really, it is they who are in "DIS-EASE" with what they have just heard. People don't know how to respond or what to say after hearing that you have suffered a great loss.

I consider myself a survivor. I know that the word survivor has different meanings for everyone. Some might think of the holocaust, or a cancer patient or someone who has been rescued from a deserted island. But they all have one thing in common. All of these people cheated death and that is exactly what widow/widowers have done. They looked death in the face and said, "You are not going to break me. I will get through this. I don't know when, but I will survive." So, going forward with the story, I will use the word "survivor" because that is what I am.

Considering everything that Mel and I had been through that last year of his life, and the most significant reminder for me should have been the preparations that went into the planning of his Celebration of Life (*I hate the word funeral*), you might wonder how I could possibly not remember that he is no longer here? Why would I set the table for two? Why would I want to call home when I know no one is there?

Those are really good and logical questions, but when dealing with the mind of a survivor you can throw logic right out the window. The brain of someone who is still grieving is in protection mode. Even though you have had a service for your spouse, your living room could be mistaken for a flower and/or card shop, your fridge is exploding with food that well wishers have dropped off but will only end up in the garbage, your heart can not comprehend that your partner is gone.

And if all that isn't enough of a reminder that you are truly alone, there is the luxury of dealing with government agencies to really finalize the passing of a loved one. Oh, let me tell you the number of times I broke down telling a complete stranger over the phone that my husband just passed away. It was easy to break down to a stranger because you didn't have to put on a front for them, plus they would never see you.

Those calls were the most difficult ones to make and I hated every minute of them. No one, nothing, can prepare you for that experience. I felt as if someone had handed me a huge eraser and said, "*Okay, start erasing Mel from all areas of life because he's not here anymore.*"

Yes, that is correct, but he still occupies a huge piece of my heart; would you like me to erase that, too? Honestly, that's how I felt calling agencies or whomever; it was simply awful.

I guess that is why they call this time the adjustment period. You have to adjust your lifestyle and routine to accommodate to a life of one. It is the most difficult thing to do and why I think there are times when your brain just goes into a lapsed stage where you do honestly forget that you are alone now because the pain of it all is just too great to bear at times.

It would even be the simplest things like grocery shopping that would make me cry. First, because Mel did all the shopping and cooking and, second, I didn't even want to eat but I knew that I had to keep my strength up so that I would not end up in the hospital myself.

Even turning on the TV or radio would scare me for the first little while. Love songs would come on that would make me fall apart, or watching TV and a commercial would come on that would make me think of Mel.

Don't get me started on movies because that was another one of our loves. We loved the classic movies or epic tales. There was also a "special" movie that meant a lot to both of us, *Bridges of Madison County,* which, even to this day, I cannot bring myself to watch when I see one of the movie channels playing it.

Adjusting is difficult; you didn't want any of it. I loved being married and knowing that someone would always be there to protect me and be a first-hand witness to my life. I loved having a warm body beside me every night. Oh sure, my family loves me and I try not to take that for granted, but the love of a spouse is something completely different.

This person saw me at my best, but, more importantly, he saw me at my worst and chose to love me anyway. This is the person who shared in my life of details and I shared in his so, yes, home life will be difficult because of the sharing that occurred between spouses. That is why radio, TV, shopping, cleaning, driving and sleeping become a scary prospect for the one left behind. You are not sure what is going to trigger a reaction so what do you do? You slowly withdraw from almost everything. You start to avoid certain things in life that you feel will cause an emotional breakdown because that particular thing has a sentimental attachment to it. Then you start realizing that almost everything reminds you of your spouse and that you need to find something new that will take your mind away for just a moment. You need a break from your memories or you'll drive yourself crazy.

I think this would be a really good time to talk about medication and/or alcohol. Drugs and alcohol are not helpful; if anything, they are very dangerous. Grief should not be treated with medications or with alcohol. Alcohol is a depressant and if there is one thing a survivor does not need in his or her life while going through this adjustment period it is something that will only bring on more depression.

As for drugs/medication, they tend to mask pain, not deal with it. My cigarette addiction was something that I was doing long before Mel passed away and I really do believe that if I had never smoked I would not have started smoking to help deal with my pain.

My only advice to someone who may be going through this adjustment period while reading this would be to feel what you need to feel in order to heal. Alcohol and drugs will only delay and hamper your healing process and I would not wish for that pain to be felt any longer than necessary for anyone grieving the loss of a loved one. This is why I refer to the one "left behind" as a survivor because if you can get through this time, all other things thrown at you in the remainder of your journey here on Earth will be like a walk in the park.

I needed to find something to occupy my mind because I was not sure what I would do or where I would end up if I didn't. I felt like I was drowning in despair and knew that I needed something to grab onto, and really fast, before it took me under. Friends and family will eventually pick up and continue on with their lives and not call you every day like they did in the beginning, and for that, you should not be upset with them because it is a reality.

You need to find that "something" for yourself to help you get through many days and months ahead. My "something" was reading. Instead of hanging out at the local corner bar (*where everybody knows your name),* my hangout became the local library. Thank HP for books. My reading, just like my journals, became my escape from reality.

Everyone needs to find their own escape when dealing with the spare time they have on their hands. Go for long walks, learn to play an instrument, enroll yourself in a night course, or take up a craft that you have always wanted to learn. Just do something that will fill your very empty days. Reading, for me, was the only outlet that gave me a reprieve from my thoughts and I welcomed it with open arms. To be able to not think about Mel and how much I missed and longed for him for a few hours at a time was a gift.

To have something else to concentrate on for awhile was a joy for me, but, of course, I also had to be careful with what I was choosing to read. I was not reading any love stories. I found myself drawn to the spiritual section of the library. I would sit there for hours reading book jackets to see if they were about what I wanted answers on.

It is unfortunate that, for most people, it takes a tragic event to make them ask the really big questions like, why are we here? Is there a God, and, if so, what is His/Her plan for me now? Is there life after death? Is there a Heaven? Will we really be reunited with our loved ones one day?

Well, let me tell you this. For every question you might have there are probably many books written on the subject. Your job will be to discover them and believe what you want to believe in, or not to believe in. Nobody can tell you what you need to believe in. The choice is yours and it always has been.

When it really comes down to it, the life that we are living is solely based on the choices that we have made along the way. You simply cannot deny that we are our life's choices, and nothing else.

I was so fortunate to be working for a company that allowed me the time that I needed when Mel's health was taking a turn for the worse. They set me up with a home office so that I could be close to Mel should he need me. After he passed, I did not return to work immediately because, quite frankly, I did not realize how exhausted and emotional I had become.

Survivors tend to neglect themselves when watching over their loved ones. The primary focus has been on your loved one for so long that you actually forget about taking care of yourself. Your sleep patterns are completely all over the board. Your eating habits go right down the toilet, and exercise? What's that? You end up operating on fumes and then, when it's all over, you will realize just how tired you really are. If you work for a company that will allow you the time to recuperate, take it, because you will need it, trust me.

It is so important to take care of your body and your mind. Now, if you happen to work for a company that, after a day or two, basically says, "Get back to work," it's time to start looking for another job, especially in this day and age. Much to my surprise, my employer extended my virtual status to continue working from home and I welcomed it. I feared going back to the office after a long absence and having people ask me how I was doing. I could envision myself breaking down right in the middle of cubicle land just because a co-worker was trying to be caring. No, staying at home for me was the answer. I simply did not want to face or be around people.

But I will let you in on something I found out first hand. Just like I was afraid of being approached by co-workers, friends and even family members asking that scary question, "So how are you doing?" I also know these people are even more apprehensive about seeing you for the first time. They just don't know what to say. They are frightened to say anything for fear of making you cry, so some might opt to not acknowledge you at all, and then they end up feeling bad because they think you will think they are heartless for not asking how you are doing. The whole first-time meetings are simply awkward for everyone because we are not conditioned and don't have any formal training in how to deal with death.

The most comforting thing that people did with me was to simply gesture, like maybe touching my hand and then saying, "I'm here if you need to talk." Something as simple as that statement lets the person know that you are thinking of them, you have not put them on the spot to answer a question about their feelings. The most important gift you have just given them is that you have offered them your time.

The highest hurdles for the survivor to clear are the loneliness and all the extra time they seem to have on their hands. And time—we lose all concept of time. It's either moving at a snail's pace or going by too fast. Survivors just don't know how we are going to fill the emptiness of our days. By offering your time to someone who has suffered a huge loss, you have thrown them a life preserver, and just in the nick of time.

The biggest adjustment during this time is in trying to find your place among the living. When looking back at my earliest journals, this was something that I consistently wrote about. Feeling lost, feeling like I didn't belong anywhere. Simply not knowing where I fit in because a big part of me was missing. Being at home made me sad, yet going out with friends or family made me feel uncomfortable. You are caught in a vicious circle. When you are out, you want to be home, and then when you are home, you want to be out. Being at home is very difficult, because everything reminds you of your spouse.

Survivors are caught in no-man's land. The home that the two of you shared and built is gone. Structurally it's there, but the heart of it is no longer beating. The experts say not to make any big decisions within the first year because you may not be thinking clearly and then end up even more depressed after you have done something major, like selling your family home, because that may not necessarily be the answer. I almost did that and let me tell you, sometimes the experts really do know what they are talking about.

Later on, I will share a story with you that will illustrate the importance of just holding back and not making rash, spur of the emotional moment decisions. I can tell you that even today, and it has been over two years since Mel passed, I still find myself, from time to time, feeling like I don't belong in certain situations. Not as much, but every once in awhile that feeling will come over me. I have been able to narrow down those events and will definitely stay away from them so that I don't feel out of place. It's really important for survivors to take note of those certain situations that might cause you discomfort or uneasiness.

If you can identify what is making you feel out of sorts, then it's your choice to not subject yourself to those situations because it is doing nothing for your recovery but only delaying the healing process.

I would have to say that on a scale of one to ten, with ten being the worst, going through your partner's clothing would have to rate as a twenty-five, or even higher. If you thought things or rooms around the house are difficult—touching, smelling, imagining and remembering your partner wearing those jeans, shirts, boxer shorts, is pretty much equivalent to torture. But by the grace of HP, I happened to have the TV on in the background one day about a week after Mel had passed. The clothes thing was nagging at me and if it had not been for this show that came on, I'm sure that Mel's clothes would still be occupying closet and shelf space in our bedroom to this day.

The topic on this show was crafts that have become popular again. One of the crafts that they were talking about was quilting but, more specifically, "Memory Quilts". Instantly I said to myself, and of course in my journal, that now I could go through Mel's clothing with a purpose. I welcomed having something new to focus on and that the end result would be that whenever I wanted to, I could wrap myself up in the quilt that I was going to make from some of Mel's clothing.

The reason I am recounting this story for you is because this was about the time I started putting more stock and faith into signs. Now maybe that was because of the books I had been reading at the time, but in my readings I remember a number of different authors talking about thoughts and how powerful they can be *(and you already know how I feel about positive thinking)*. The constant message that was repeated in most of my books was that if you really and truly think about something long enough you will get answers to your questions, the solutions to your problems. Thoughts can be that powerful. If you honestly believe in your thoughts, the universe will respond.

An example of the universe working its magic is when you hear people saying things like, "What a coincidence", "Talk about being in the right place at the right time", or even better yet, "It was like a miracle."

Well, I am going to dispel all of those frequently used phrases and simply say, "Ask and you shall receive." There are no coincidences or accidents in life. You are in the right place at the right time every minute of your life. We are exactly where we are supposed to be and we are meeting the people we are supposed to meet. We are attracting everything that happens in our life with our thoughts, good and bad.

How many times have we heard the saying, "Be careful what you wish for"? Think about that one for a minute. Do you really think it was a coincidence to have the TV on to a program that I have never watched in my entire life and it happened to address the nagging issue of Mel's clothes?

Do you really think it was an accident that I went back to the hospital to meet Mel's cousin and then that little miracle happens outside with the seagull?

When something good or bad happens to me, I usually go back and think about what I may have done or, more specifically, what thoughts was I putting out there for this to have happened? It was my "choice" to leave the TV on. It was my "choice" to go back to the hospital.

On average, a person will make 2000 choices daily. Think about that. You make 2000 choices every day. I don't know about you, but when I heard that statistic, it just blew me away. So then I started to think more about it and you know what? I think those experts are right again *(hence the reason they are called experts)* because I thought, *"Okay, I choose what time I am going to get up every day, then I choose whether or not to shower and then, if I do, I choose to either wash my hair, put conditioner in it, shave my armpits, and do I do my legs as well? Hang on a second. I might even make more than 2000 choices a day because I have only been out of bed for ten minutes and have already made four or five choices—in the shower of all places—and I have not even left the house. Unbelievable! Can you imagine how many more choices I am actually going to make once I wash the sleep out of my eyes and really wake up and start my day?"*

I know, I'm being a smart ass and making fun of the experts and their studies but, really, do you see from my lame example how we can choose anything, anything we want?

Think about some of the routines, or ruts, that we tend to complain about from time to time. Are they really routines or our daily choices? We blindly do the same things over and over again not realizing that what we consider everyday events are really choices. So, if you want to get out of the rut you find yourself in, STOP, and choose something different, then there will be no more routine. You are not blindly going through your day when you choose to change your routine. You choose to put yourself into the driver's seat of your life and take yourself off autopilot.

Here's an experiment. One day, probably on a weekend so you don't end up in Yahoopitsville and late for work, consciously do the opposite of what you would normally do and see where that will take you. I can guarantee you won't have the same day you had yesterday. Who knows, you might end up having the greatest day of your life because you chose differently.

Think about that for one moment. If we consciously choose something different every day, can you imagine how exciting it would be to wake up every morning anticipating what kind of day will unfold right before your eyes, just because you have made different choices? Will it be better or worse, dull or exciting, the same or new? Oh my, it almost sounds as though my life could be filled with adventures instead of the mundane!

So then, what is stopping us from choosing differently every day? Nothing! Well, that's not entirely true. You are stopping this from happening. We all are. Nobody is forcing us to do anything. It's all our choices. It's all up to us and always has been. About mid-way through 2006, I decided to be more consciously aware of my choices because it is my right to do so. At first it was difficult, but it's like any type of training or practicing. It's always hard to start but if you keep working at it, it becomes easier and you start seeing different results. When you see new results from making different choices, you will start to believe that anything is possible. You face the day with excitement instead of dread or boredom. You start to think that if you really put your mind to it, you could really change the direction of your life. You begin to think that anything is possible. You might actually convince yourself that you can write a book that could possibly help just one person, and get it published. Now, wouldn't that be crazy?

I will give you an example of what the experts were talking about when stating that after someone has suffered a huge loss they should not make any big purchases or moves within the first year of adjusting to life without their significant other.

Weekends in the summer were proving to be very difficult for me. I would be driving around and I would see campers, RVs, trucks pulling pop-up trailers and I would get very emotional. I knew that I would miss camping, fishing, bonfires—everything about the great outdoors, but not to the extent that I was. This was a life that Mel introduced me to and that I grew to love more and more every year that we did it. Now I had nothing. All I had was my condo and the thought of sitting home every weekend was depressing me even more than I can describe to you at this time.

My neighbours have a cabin and when I would see them packing up for the weekend, I would become jealous, even a bit angry. This was not good because, if anything, it was making me hate my home, our home, even more. I remember writing in my journals how much I missed our special getaway weekends. How I looked forward to us hitting the highway every Friday afternoon, heading for the lake to enjoy the weekend surrounded by nature.

I remember asking the universe to help me get through this. I started to think that I would go through the "Buy and Sell" catalogue and perhaps look at purchasing a small pop-up trailer. Yes! This is what I was going to do.

I was feeling pretty positive about this decision and then something happened. The universe had other ideas about how to solve my problem. All I had to do was take a chance.

I made a call to Rick, our funeral director, because I wanted to settle my bill with him. He ended up becoming such a good friend to me that we started talking about a lot of other things, as we usually did whenever we got on the phone. Rick asked me how I was doing and I told him about my struggles with the whole camping thing and how I had just made a decision to look for a pop-up trailer. I told him that I needed something to help pass the time on the long summer weekends ahead of me, which I was realistically going to have to face on my own.

Ideally, I wanted a cabin at a lake somewhere, but my lottery had not come in, so you do what you have to do in order to keep your sanity.

Rick knew that camping was a big part of my life with Mel and could definitely understand my frustration, and then he mentioned something to me. He actually laughed and said that my timing was impeccable, or was it? Talk about a small world, and again, there are no coincidences, but just before I had called him, the man who made the DVD for Mel's service was in his office and they were chatting about things. One of the things that they were talking about was the fact that he and his wife were getting ready to sell their family cottage/trailer that they had owned for the last twelve years.

Rick continued to tell me more about the trailer and that they had not been using it as much in the past few years, the condition of it, and where it was located. The location was a sign that maybe this place was meant to be mine. It was where Mel had taken me to fish for the very first time in my life. So, without getting sentimental and crazy, I phoned the family and told them that Rick and I had spoken and that I was interested in seeing the summer home they were selling.

To make a long story short, I brought Hayley and her boyfriend, Russ, with me to check it out. I wanted Russ to look it over to make sure it was structurally sound before I made an offer, if that was even going to happen at all. The trailer had obviously been maintained and cared for with a lot of love and hard work. The place just felt right and the couple instantly had a good feeling about selling the place to me. They had other offers in, but for some reason, they held off selling to the interested parties. They wanted to ensure they were selling to someone who would love and care for it just as much as they had over the years.

I remember the woman said as soon as she saw my face that she knew I was going to be the new owner of a place that held so many happy memories for her and her family. You could almost say they were waiting for me to show up on their doorstep.

I ended up getting the place for a steal; family and friends could not believe my good fortune. This little treasure fell into my lap at a time when I truly wished for it. This was not good fortune, this was not fate. This was the universe working its magic for me yet again. I was absolutely sure of it and was starting to feel something inside me change. I knew that HP existed and was always there looking out for me. All I had to do was believe.

Here is an excellent example of ask and you shall receive. I wanted, no, just wait, I *needed* this place to help me with my recovery. This trailer has meant the world to me since. It has been a gift and such a source of pleasure for me. I know the spirit of Mel is all around this little gem. It's not much, but it's all mine. If it were not for Mel, I would not have bought this place. I have never felt so connected to Mel as I do when I am here.

I know that it sounds ridiculous because Mel had never even set foot into the trailer but it's in the energy around this place that I feel his presence and his blessing. We had talked about looking for a summer place because the camper, even though we loved it, was getting to be very costly to upkeep, especially with the soaring price of gasoline.

Had Mel been alive and had we found this place on our own, or something close to it, I know he would have been in his glory. I know that he most likely would have lived out there all week long during the summer with our cat, Mocha, and I would have come out every weekend to be with them. I could see him tinkering around the place and fishing every single day—rain or shine.

Something important happened when I took possession of the trailer that very first weekend. When I was moving things in to make it more of my own place, I was looking around for something else that I seemed to have forgotten to bring with me. Now what was it? It was nagging at me until I realized that it wasn't something that I had forgotten. It was that someone was missing.

I remember sitting down and crying like a baby, but it was something that needed to happen. This breakdown taught me something very valuable. My new summer getaway home had absolutely no connection to Mel whatsoever, except in spirit, yet I was missing him there.

The lesson I learned and want to share with you is this: If I thought that selling my condo and moving into some place new that held no memories would make me miss Mel less, I was absolutely kidding myself. The purchasing of the trailer proved that it would not make any difference where I called home.

This experience most likely ended up saving me thousands of dollars, or even more, because the housing market had just started going through the roof. If I needed a change, moving was not the answer. Renovations and painting would be my solution to my home dilemma for now. If, after doing what I could do cosmetically to our home I still felt depressed because of the memories, then, and only then, would I seriously consider selling and finding a new place to call home.

So the experts had it right yet again. I think if I had acted solely on my emotional state at the time and sold my condo, I would have ended up in a financial mess that would have only added to my depression and caused me unnecessary stress, which I just could not afford emotionally at that time in my recovery.

Move for practical reasons—downsize to save money, move to a safer neighbourhood, but, if you are moving to run away from memories, guess what? They come with you wherever you go, and thank God for them.

I had invited my sister Debi and my nieces out that first weekend at the trailer to help christen my new summer home. We had a wonderful time and it was good to be surrounded with family who loved me and, more importantly, would not allow me to be alone and who wanted to share in my new-found happiness.

On my drive home that Sunday evening I remember listening to my jazz station and thinking to myself, "*I wonder if Mel would be happy and would have approved of my decision to buy this place.*" No sooner did I finish thinking that than I happened to look up towards the sky, because it looked as though it may start to rain, and saw the most amazing formation of clouds directly in front of me. I could clearly see a face with a huge smile staring back at me. I couldn't believe it, and then I quickly remembered that I was actually driving a vehicle at 110 kilometres per hour and better get my eyes back on the road.

But I was amazed and a little freaked out at what I was seeing. How I wished someone else were in the car to witness it with me. But it didn't matter because I got my answer to my question loud and clear. Then the tears started to run down my face as I continued to drive down the highway back to the city.

For the first time in a long time, I couldn't wait to finally get home. I didn't feel alone that night. I knew that Mel was with me. I mean, who could deny that? He had just smiled at me from heaven, was guiding me back home, and was letting me know that he was happy for me and my new-found treasure.

Chapter Eight

In Case of Emergency

Looking back on my choice to purchase the little trailer and piece of property to enjoy by myself, or with family and friends, well, let's just say I am not sure what I would have done that first summer without it. It became my private sanctuary, a place where I could go to get away from old memories and from the past. Even though it was a new place never shared with Mel, I was more connected to Mel there than in our own home. Perhaps it was because it was out in the country and away from the city. Both of our roots were in the country and we had known that, one day, we would return to it.

When I was out at the trailer, everywhere I looked nature was all around me. It was Mel who showed me how beautiful nature is and taught me to never take it for granted. Being at home was proving to be more difficult as the months went by, so being able to go some place new and beautiful was a saving grace for me.

I knew I was going to have to learn how to start getting through the "firsts" without falling apart. My first hurdle would be vacation time. What would I do with myself for three weeks?

Would I even be able to stand myself for that long? There was no getting away from it, I would have to endure the time away from work and go and try to enjoy myself on vacation. I made sure I had lots of reading material, projects to do around the trailer, movies I wanted to watch, and friends and family to join me on the weekends.

It sounded like a great plan but it was so terribly difficult, especially during the nights. God how I missed Mel! I just kept thinking how much he would have loved this place and how much fun we would have had together. Thank goodness I brought my journal(s) because I could pour my guts into them. Everything I was feeling, missing and wishing for was written down. I cannot tell you how much comfort my journals gave to me during this adjustment time. They allowed me to get my thoughts out instead of keeping them all bottled up inside. I was never alone because they had become my friends. I did not always want to share my feelings with family and friends all the time, for fear that they would turn to me and say, "Oh, just get over it, Kim. Dwelling on the past isn't going to help you recover."

I know you think that sounds ridiculous because who would ever say something like that to a grieving spouse? Well, believe it, because it actually happened to me. When the words "Just get over it" came out I was completely dumbfounded and so incredibly shocked that I actually thought I had heard wrong. It was like a slap across the face. Here I thought I was doing so well considering my heart had been sucked out of my body. I was making a concerted effort not to burden people, so I wasn't calling them as much as I really wanted to.

The circumstances around this conversation were that I had made plans to get together at my trailer with some of Mel's relatives, have some drinks, food, and a night of games and laughter. When I found out that they had double booked and couldn't make it out after all, I was disappointed for a couple reasons. One, it took a lot of going back and forth to hammer out a day that would work for everyone. Two, I was so looking forward to having Mel's family around me because it had been awhile since I had seen anyone from his side of the family. Did they not understand what I was going through and why I was so upset? All I was asking for was one stinking evening out of their busy schedules to spend some time with me. They couldn't break their plans just this once? I guess not.

Then I remembered getting a package from Linda that contained many writings, articles and poems about grieving and remembered there was something in there that dealt specifically with just that kind of statement. It basically said that if someone tells a survivor to "just get over it," it's usually for one of two reasons.

First, they, too, are having a very difficult time dealing with the loss of this person and the surviving spouse is a constant reminder of the person who has passed, making it difficult to spend time with them.

Secondly, and most likely, they want the survivor to be their old self again because they just don't know how to deal with this new person who now stands in front of them. They enjoyed and liked being with the "old Kim". They are very uncomfortable being around this new person, this stranger. They fear that they might say something that might spark a memory that could cause them to break down and that is something that they cannot deal with, because they have not allowed themselves to break down and cry. So they distance themselves from the survivor.

The experts say that this response usually comes from a male friend or family member, and in my case the experts were right. As humans, we just don't know how to grieve and, unfortunately, men have a harder time with it. Many men feel that showing any type of emotion is a sign of weakness and that they have to be strong for others. They never really mourn properly for the people who meant so much to them, so they become hardened in a way, and expect that grieving should only last for a certain amount of time. Well, I'm here to tell you there is no timetable for when a person should get over it.

Everyone deals with grief differently and that's what everyone needs to understand. If it takes only a few weeks or months for the survivor to move forward, don't judge them. It doesn't mean that they loved their spouse any less than the person who is still mourning years later. We all heal and cope differently. There is no quick fix for someone going through the loss of a loved one. They have to feel what they need to feel. The loss of a grandparent, an aunt or uncle, a friend, a sibling or a parent is different for everyone because it's about the relationship, the bond they shared with that individual.

Now there is one type of loss I purposely left out and that is the loss of a child. Even having lived through dealing with the loss of a spouse, who was incredibly loved and adored, I can't even begin to imagine a parent dealing with the loss of their child. There can be no greater loss than that, because it defies the natural progression of life. It just doesn't make sense, or does it? Why was this soul given to us for such a short period of time just to be taken away? It simply defies logic and reason and that's why we can't wrap our minds around such a loss.

Kiminition: on the loss of a child:

This is where you, as the parent, have to dig deep and do your own search for answers or you will just wallow in your grief. I truly believe that HP only gives to those whom He/She feels can persevere and wants you to learn something of the greatest value by giving you the hardest life lesson that there is to learn—how to continue to live life and carry on when you have lost your child. Should you choose never to search for those answers as to why this child came into your life, and make sense of what that life meant to you, then that is your choice. But I think that HP chose you (Yes, you were the chosen one) specifically because he knew that you would find those answers and would find a way to continue living a meaningful life and truly become an inspiration to others.

I had invited one of my girlfriends, Sherry, to come out and spend a weekend with me at the trailer and just have some girl time. Sherry is a single mom of two and I knew that she would enjoy the quiet, relaxing time away from the city, work and the kids. But as it turned out, it was a strange weekend.

We had a terrible rainstorm on the Saturday evening and it pretty much carried over to the Sunday. Trees were down because of high winds, branches were all over the place and power was sporadically on and off. I considered myself very lucky because I was sitting on high ground while other areas were completely under water. But life is filled with nothing but yin and yang. I was lucky that my trailer was safe, but me, on the other hand, no—not so lucky.

Approximately a year prior to this, my cat, Mocha, whom Mel had given to me as a birthday present one year, had accidentally stabbed my eye with his claw when we were lying in bed. During this particular weekend, that same eye was giving me problems. So much so that not only did the rainstorm keep me up all night, but the pain and constant tearing of that one eye almost drove me right through the roof.

When Sherry saw how puffy and irritated my eye was in the morning, we decided that I needed to go to emergency. The thought of stepping foot into a hospital made me nauseous, but I simply had no choice. Something was terribly wrong and I needed to get it checked out.

We drove to the nearest hospital and, of course, had to go to the admissions desk in emergency before a doctor would see me. Well, you know the drill. You have to fill out a form with all the particulars but the admissions clerk could see that I was in no shape to write so she verbally asked me for my information. That poor clerk, she was only doing her job but I simply fell apart when she asked me for my husband's name.

She just assumed I was married because I was still wearing my wedding ring.

Once I regained my composure and told her that he had recently passed away, of course she felt terrible. We then continued on with the remainder of the form. She asked me who the contact for my "in case of emergency" was and I completely broke down again. Thank goodness Sherry was there to finish speaking for me because I just could not get the words out. I had to think about that question for a bit. It's that whole form thing again—widow, in case of emergency—constant reminders to let you know, just in case you forgot for one moment, that you're alone and nobody is there for you. I know that's not true today, but right at that moment and with Mel's passing still so fresh, that interaction in the emergency department pretty much killed me. I was just a bundle of emotions. I was feeling sorry for myself because of my stupid eye, I was feeling bad that I ruined the weekend for Sherry, and I felt terrible for making that clerk feel so sorry for me just because she was doing me a favour by filling out the form on my behalf.

But the one good thing that came out of that visit was that because of my emotional outbursts I got to see a doctor right away. *(Sure, they wanted one less crazy person out of their waiting room and out of the hospital as soon as possible.)*

The experience got me to thinking that I would have to go through it again with other forms and notifications at work, with utility companies, the bank, insurance companies, and my will. Everyone would need to know that my emergency contact, my beneficiary, my soul mate was gone. *(Here comes that big old eraser again; I was being forced to eradicate Mel from my past almost as though he didn't exist and that pissed me off.)* So now you have to go through the process of figuring out whose name you can put on forms. Someone who won't mind dropping everything they are doing should you need them because of an emergency, who won't mind being woken up at three in the morning because there has been an accident, who will be burdened with you simply because you decided to put their name down on a piece paper where asked, "contact name in case of emergency."

A word of advice, don't assume the person you are going to write down will view it as an honour that you selected them from among all the other people in your life. Let them know, and honestly ask them if they would take it on and not hate you for it. This is something not to be taken lightly and the person you have chosen should be notified so they are not caught off guard.

The reason I bring this up is that people will surprise you, and not necessarily always in good ways. You will get support from unexpected places and people and these people will remain very special to you. They, perhaps, will never know the depth of your gratitude for the support they offered you at a time that was filled with so many unknowns. I just assumed that some people in my life would be there for me no matter what, but I was wrong. As I stated earlier, some people are very uncomfortable with having to deal with the unfamiliar, the unknown, and simply don't want things to change. They want you to just miraculously continue with your old life the way it used to be.

But I, too, was waiting for that, wondering when I was going to feel normal again. I mean, come on, it had already been months. When was the old Kim going to come back? I could see that certain people were also waiting for the return of that person. They wanted things to get back to normal, more so for themselves than for me. I was feeling pressure to hurry up so that I could make them feel better, and then I snapped out of it and thought to myself, "*Wait a minute here. I am never going to be the same person I was. How can I be? I was a different person before Mel, again while I was with him, and now I will definitely be a different person without my husband. I will have to find my new normal, my new self, and that will take time. How much time? I haven't got a clue, so don't rush me!*"

When I came to that realization, and also had it confirmed by Linda that I would never be that person again took away the pressure and it made where I was in my recovery okay. It also showed me that certain people in my life needed me to be strong for them in order to make the friendship comfortable, to be able to be their sounding board, their voice of reason and to hear about their problems. Hang on a second! What about me? How about being there for me?

I remember being disappointed with some individuals because I was turning to them in my time of need, yet they were continuing to dump on me and ask me for my opinions on what they should do with their lives. Was this how our relationship always had been? Was I only now seeing what my role was? Friendship should be a give-and-take relationship, should it not? I was now seeing that some of my friendships worked well when I was on the giving end as opposed to being on the receiving end. I didn't want to solve their problems anymore because I had enough on my plate at the moment. If a true friend could not see that I was still hurting and lost myself, then was it a relationship worth saving? I was still trying to find my way, my footing again. And really, I only wished they could try my problems on for a short time to see what real problems felt like.

What I learned in the years shared with Mel was that living life uncomplicated was the way that I needed to continue living going forward. I needed to be mindful and focus on me and my recovery. If that meant saying goodbye to relationships that were one-sided and unhealthy, then so be it. I did it once before, so doing it with some friends and family members would not be as difficult as it was to say goodbye to Mark all those years ago. Unfortunately, or fortunately, it all depends on how you look at it.

It took this life-changing event in my life to make me examine some of my relationships. I was in the driver's seat of my life and this was the route that I decided I needed to take. Here I was again having to make some difficult choices when it came to relationships, yet I knew in my heart that these were the right choices for me. To move forward, I would have to say goodbye, for now, to those who were bringing me down. I wanted to surround myself with people who continually attracted positive things into their lives and who made good choices for themselves and for their families. I needed to focus on getting better myself and not be burdened with other people's problems, especially when most of their problems were self-induced because of the choices they continued to make.

I am really happy to say I have grown from this experience because I no longer harbor any ill will toward these individuals. They are who they are and I have to accept that it is not my job to change them, and not for me to hold any resentment toward them. They were in my life for a reason and I am thankful for what they have taught me.

I continued to face other firsts: Mel's birthday, my birthday, Christmas, our anniversary and New Year's Eve. The people who really love you will not leave you alone and will want to be there for you during these times. It's okay to want to be alone if that is what you choose. I know that for Mel's birthday, I chose to be alone to acknowledge that day in my own special way.

As for the other occasions, I could not stomach the thought of being alone, especially during Christmas because that holiday is all about family. This is where family and close friends really come into play. Make new plans and new memories to get through those particular holidays; it worked for me. Holidays can be difficult at the best of times, so coming up with an alternate plan, or perhaps doing something you have never done before to get through the "firsts" without your partner is something you need to do.

This year will be the third set of holidays I will not be able to share with Mel. But it's okay now, because I am already looking forward to spending it with my brother, Fred, and his wife, Denise, my sisters, who will also travel to Fred and Denise's because we have started a new tradition. I am so thankful to have the love of my family around me in order to help create a new tradition. I am not sure that Fred and Denise realize what their home means to me during this time. Not only is the holiday Christmas and New Year's Eve, but our wedding anniversary is also right smack dab in the middle of it all. To have an escape and to focus on something new is my safe haven during that time of year.

Chapter Nine

Land of the Living

Halleluiah! I made it through the holidays! It was 2006 and I made a promise to myself (not a resolution), an honest to goodness promise. This year was definitely going to be better than the past year. I couldn't make any guarantees, but I would try much harder to begin to enjoy life again.

What did I mean by that? Well, I would start by not wishing I was dead or thinking about my own mortality as much as I was. Oh yes. I couldn't believe that I had actually been thinking of my own demise on a regular basis. Depression was something that I was now battling, but I would not give in to it. Yet, I was thinking things like, what will be my fate? When is HP going to call me home? So many things happened to me when Mel passed—I mean, right there in that room, the minute he took his last breath. I was in total shock that my husband was no longer alive. He was no longer mine to have and to hold. He was onto something bigger and better, his next great adventure. But before he left this world, he gave me one last gift. He had one last lesson to teach me, and again, I was the eager student ready to take mental notes. He showed me that death is beautiful and that you don't have to be afraid of it. He showed me that dying is dignified and regal. My God, what a gift!

Perhaps it was because of this gift that I was no longer afraid of death. Because I no longer had a fear of death, I allowed myself to think about how my end would come, and to ask for it to come soon. I would say to myself during this time, "Oh *please God, take me out of this misery now. I don't think I am going to make it, but more importantly, I don't know if I want to make it. It's terrible living with no dreams or hopes.*"

Something inside me at that very moment told me something was definitely wrong. Mel had taught me something much more important than not fearing death; he also taught me how to live life passionately and with meaning. I needed help to get back to where I had been. I wanted to believe in something again. I wanted to believe in me again. I needed to know that I was going to come out of this situation a better and stronger person than ever before. But I couldn't do it alone. I needed help and asking for help has always been difficult for me. But I don't think I am alone in this. Most people have a tough time asking others for help because they view it as a weakness, perhaps even bordering on pathetic. I didn't care about what other people thought. My recovery was too important, so I was just going to have to swallow my pride and ask for help anyway. I could not go on existing as I was, so I called Linda. She agreed that perhaps it was time I joined a bereavement group. This would end up becoming a place where I felt I really belonged. I finally got my wish, the same wish I had the day I left the hospital for the last time when I wanted everyone to feel what I was feeling. The answer to my wish came in the form of eight other surviving women I would come to know, admire and learn from. I was no longer alone. I was no longer a freak. There were others just like me, other women who were merely existing, and no longer living and enjoying life.

It was during this same time that I had started to paint and renovate my condo. I needed to change the look but still incorporate

Mel into the new surroundings. I am so happy to this day that there are reminders of him throughout our home. Some things would not even be recognizable to some, but to me they are there for a reason.

The planning and shopping gave me something new to focus on. Between working, going to bereavement classes, my sporting activities, reading and home renovations, my mind was completely occupied during the days. But the nights! The nights were and still are the hardest to get through. I would turn to my journal and write to Mel.

It was around this time that I was really starting to struggle with the loneliness. What was I going to do? What were my options at this point, besides taking matters literally into my own hands? I could no longer deny it. There was still nothing better than the sensation of human touch, of that kiss that rocks your world.

I remember saying to Mel that if he didn't like what I was writing in the journal about the idea of having sex with someone other than him, he had no one to blame but himself. He was the one who taught me how to open up, to be proud of my body, to not be inhibited. He taught me that if making love is with someone you respect, trust, love and truly treasure, it's magical. It's so absolutely delicious you almost feel that it must be illegal because anything that good has to be wrong—right?

But it still didn't seem right to be having thoughts of sex without Mel. I felt, in a sick sort of way, that I would be cheating on him. But I had to face facts. I was alive with so much living still to do. To deny those feelings would be ridiculous. The memory of what Mel said to me about not being a martyr came back to me when my mind would go down this path. He knew that I would love again, but it was still an uncomfortable fact for me to comprehend. The possibility of starting a new relationship, a sexual one, is a really hard one to deal with. All I can say is that when you are ready, you will know it. It will most likely happen again and, when it does, don't turn your back on it because "it" is what makes you feel alive and human.

I had to keep my promise to myself and to Mel. I had been writing in my journal that I knew Mel was looking down on me and that he was most likely disappointed with how I was choosing to live my life without him. It was so hard to pretend that I was getting better when really it was just a constant struggle to get myself out of bed every day. Do you believe it? Just getting showered and dressed was a huge success for me back then.

I knew I had to leave the safety and comfort of my own home. I could no longer avoid co-workers, friends and family. I had to suck it up and start making myself part of the living. I did this by asking my employer if I could come back to the office, start off a couple of days a week, and slowly condition myself to the point where it was back in the office five days a week.

The transition was great. There were no awkward moments with co-workers because it had almost been a year and they had seen me from time to time already. Of course, back in the office, pajamas and sweats were not considered business attire. It was only when I started to go through my work clothes that I realized I had lost weight, a lot of weight. It's funny how you completely forget about your personal appearance. Well, when you have no one, including yourself, to get all pretty for, what's the point? So then I started to really look at myself in the mirror for the first time in a long time. I had that same feeling rush over me all over again from all those years ago. Who is that looking back at me from the mirror? I don't know who that person is. *Oh my God, not this again.* I didn't want to go back to that old, negative, unbreakable person. I didn't want this experience to turn me into a bitter and angry woman. I knew logically that it was not possible because I had come too far.

The best years of my life to that point were my years with Mel. Something significant and life changing happened to me during those precious years and I was not going to allow myself to back slide. I was not going to allow death to make me a victim. Instead, I thought that if Mel were looking down on me I would make him proud so that he could point down to me to show all his buddies that I was his wife and that I was doing well all on my own. I knew what I needed to do. I needed to work on changing the reflection staring back at me to someone I could be proud of once again.

In my journals, I started to write about myself and who I was at this point in my life. I reflected on my accomplishments over the last year without Mel. I was totally amazed that I had made it this far. That in itself was an enormous accomplishment, because there were times when I was so close to rock bottom it scared me. But something inside me got me through yet another day in my recovery process. I now know that it was my inner voice, my higher self. The conversations that I was having with myself were positive and uplifting. I was constantly picking myself up and acting like my own personal cheerleader. I convinced myself that if I was able to get through that year, going forward would be a piece of cake.

I can trace the second awakening in my lifetime back to an event that happened in the summer of 2006 that made me stop and say, "*Okay Kim, you're done with your mourning for Mel.*" That event was skydiving. It came about one Friday evening after work when I was with my very special group of friends. *(They don't know it, but I call them my "life-timers".)*

JP, one of my life-timers, threw out the question as we were sitting outside having a drink. "Would anybody be interested in jumping out of a plane?"

I had to think about it for only a millisecond and then said to count me in. It was something I had always wanted to do but never had the courage to do because I was afraid of the risk. I was tempting fate. Well, you know how I feel about that now. I no longer feared death and felt much lighter as a result. Why put off things you want to do because of fears? That's no way to live.

Now, I am not saying to start taking ridiculous risks, like running into a burning building to save a salami sandwich that you just made. That's not it at all. Common sense should always prevail, but my point here is this: What are we all waiting for?

If there is something inside of you that you have always wanted to do, come up with a plan of how to make it happen. I'm not only talking about events like skydiving. I am talking about the everyday events. If you want a different career, to live in another neighbourhood or city, buy a brand new vehicle, a cottage, meet new friends, take up a sport, learn a different language or, even more drastic, cut ties with people who are holding you back or making you feel bad about yourself, do it! These are just some examples of what I am talking about. It may be time to start being mindful and doing things for yourself instead of others for a change. Please don't live by my example and wait for someone so precious to you to either get sick or pass away to make you realize just how little time we have here to do it right.

The day of my jump came and I was neither scared nor excited. I was very calm about the whole thing, because I knew it was going to be an incredible experience, one I would never forget. And I was not disappointed. My tandem partner, who has taken a lot of jumpers throughout his twenty-year career, commented on how relaxed I was. I was not going to get into the whole, *"Well, it's because I am not afraid to die thing."* I was just ready to do something that I have always wanted to do and did not realize that the end result would be my first step to officially moving forward and continuing on with my life's journey. Jumping out of a plane made me finally realize that I was still alive and had so much more living to do. Talk about literally taking a leap of faith. I am so grateful for these gifts that continually come my way.

From that day on, I had a renewed excitement about life, about my life, realizing how I am in total control of what happens in it. There is no one else navigating my life's path, I am the one manifesting my reality. I am the one making my choices, good and bad. I have so much to be grateful for that my heart is overflowing with love. I am at peace with myself and I can honestly say, for the first time in my life, at the ripe young age of forty-four, I really like myself and am very proud of where I am today.

My life seemed to be on the right road again, only there was one thing missing. I felt that I was ready to have someone share in my life again; to what degree, I was not sure. There, I said it, and it took sixteen months for it to happen but it was the only nagging issue in my life. This is where my journals and my positive talk came into major play.

Earlier, I said that when you are ready you will know it. Life and life situations can never be forced, planned or scripted. They just have to unfold the way they were meant to. I had been writing in my journals about an upcoming baseball tournament I was wavering on even attending. I did not want to take time away from my precious weekends out at the trailer, but I had also promised that I would make a better effort to join in on more activities with friends. If I were going to meet someone, how could that possibly happen when I was constantly in hibernation mode.

I bit the bullet and committed myself to playing in this out-of-town weekend baseball tournament. My choice was to spend time at my trailer during the evenings and not tent with my friends, but instead, wake up early in the mornings and drive in for the day's scheduled games. Deep down inside I knew that I would have a good time, because I was surrounded by friends who love me and really wanted me there.

But I also provided myself with an out so that if those feelings of "not belonging" popped up because my friends are mostly couples, I could escape to my trailer and not have to subject myself to feeling out of place. You always have to have a Plan B when you are starting to rejoin society, just in case you have to bail out.

We were there early Saturday morning getting ready to play our first game. While getting our gear on and going through the warm up, I overheard a conversation about us waiting for another player to show up. This was news to me because I did not realize that we did not have enough players for the weekend, but then I really did not give it much more thought after that. This person was coming only to help us out for the Saturday, because we would have enough players for the Sunday games.

We had already played an inning or two when my girlfriend, Hayley, noticed this man walking towards us and said to me, "Oh my, look what the cat dragged in. He is good looking, Kim." I just laughed and did not pay much attention to Hayley's comment, or to this stranger, who would become a special friend to me over the next few weeks.

The weather was taking a turn for the worse and all the players needed to take shelter in the arena quickly because conditions were hitting almost tornado proportions. We all sat around playing cards, having a few drinks, laughing and talking like we always do. Hayley, God love her, kept on jabbing me in the side and throwing comments my way about this new stranger among us. She was a busy little beaver and found out more details about this potential prospect. Looks were a given. Steve's eyes were absolutely hypnotizing and he had a smile that shone. You could tell he was in very good physical shape.

Intelligence, well let's just say, Steve's IQ was bordering on genius. And the best of all, if you could believe it, he was single. But the most alluring quality about him was his quick wit and fantastic sense of humour. Laughing is so important to me. It keeps you young at heart and is the best medicine for anything ailing you.

I wanted to strike up a conversation with Steve to see if there would even be a connection. The conversation between us seemed natural and easy. We made each other laugh and that was good. The weather eventually cleared and we were able to finish off our game for the day. My plan was to head back to my trailer after the games and not join my friends back at their campsite because of the long drive ahead of me but something, or should I say, someone quickly made me change my mind. I couldn't believe how schoolgirlish I was becoming over the prospect of continuing a conversation with Steve, should he decide to come back to my friends' campsite. I was hoping he would and, as fate would have it (or the universe made it happen), he decided to join us. He was going to delay heading out for the long drive ahead of him as well to finish other obligations he had previously made for this same weekend.

We had the opportunity to talk to one another again by the waterfalls at the campsite. It was very peaceful and private. I felt a connection with Steve but, because it had been awhile, I did not want to read anything into this pleasant and unexpected encounter. As it turned out, my friend, Mike, who had invited Steve to join us that day, happened to mention that Steve was interested in me as well. *What? Did you mean me or was he actually looking at someone else who was standing behind me?*

I was shocked because I already knew going into this that there was an age difference, and the difference was not something that I would have particularly chosen in a partner. Steve was much younger than me, but then I thought, break away from old habits and misconceptions. Do not judge a book by its cover. I had been writing in my journal over the previous few weeks about how, if given the opportunity again, my next partner would have to be funny, healthy, attractive, independent, respectful, enjoy what he did for a living, enjoy life and the adventure of it, but most importantly, that he would have a good heart. So if I met someone who filled those requirements would I really hold back because of age? I don't think so. Age has always just been numbers to me anyway. It's how people conduct themselves as individuals that matters to me. If you are embarrassed to be seen with someone out in public—guess what—don't be with them in private either.

Remember that email my sister Rose sent me? The one about why people come into our lives? It arrived about this time. That message has been so helpful to me because it is so true. Steve came into my life for a reason. His role in my life was a short one and that's all it was ever meant to be. He showed me that I was ready to love again and that I would be okay with it. The ground would not open up and swallow me whole. Steve holds a very special place in my heart for the gift he gave me.

Life goes on whether we want to admit it or not. Human beings were not designed to go through life alone. We need that human contact and interaction. Mel's last words came back to me and always made me smile. He knew better than I at the time that I would eventually let someone else in. He was so right, and I am telling you right now, I don't want to go through life by myself.

Now, let's not get this confused with needing someone. I don't need someone to make me feel complete or to look after me. That's not it at all. I *want* to invite someone into my life, share in my successes, joys, sorrows, laughter and, most importantly, in my love, as I want to share in theirs.

Do I want marriage again? I don't know. I don't think so, but something very important I have learned during my recovery time is that I try to avoid using the word "never". I said that I would never love again after Mel. Well, look at what I have been talking about for the last few pages. You don't know what is waiting around the corner for you until you decide to make the choice to have a look for yourself.

Chapter Ten

My Season

Where would we be without our friends, the people who have become our chosen families and, in some cases, actually end up being closer to us than some of our own blood relatives?

I was fortunate to define at a very young age what true friendship really meant to me. When looking back on my younger days, I don't have bad memories about being hurt by people I considered my closest or best friends. No. I was lucky in that I have always chosen my friends wisely and because of that selection process my group has always been small and intimate. That is absolutely fine with me, quality not quantity.

The special people I continue to surround myself with are people with whom I would trust with my life. They are the ones who will be there for me no matter what and I don't have to question their loyalty—kind of an unwritten agreement that I inherently know that we have each other's back. They will be honest and supportive of what I do and truly have my best interest at heart. They want nothing but the best for me and want to see me succeed, and I want the same for them. Those are the types of friends I hold close to my heart. The ones who do not share my ideals about friendship? Well, I call these people acquaintances and will not confuse the two. It is much safer that way.

Lori, who is one of these special friends I absolutely adore, had invited me to a party she was hosting for one of her dearest friends, Tom, who was leaving the city for something bigger and better. I knew Tom as well so I was one of the guests who was invited to wish him well as he was about to start on a new chapter in his life. How exciting for him! As usual, Lori's party was a huge success and everyone had a wonderful time. About mid-evening, after Lori served us a delicious meal, we were all sitting around having drinks. I was talking with Tom and another friend, Gerry. We were chatting about something when, out of the blue, Tom said he had a great idea. Gerry and I were curious so we sat there with great anticipation, and then he said it out loud. He had the perfect man in mind for me! I have absolutely no idea how we got from the previous topic to matchmaking 101! Had someone just dropped a funny pill in my wine without my noticing, or was I was simply caught up in the pleasant atmosphere the evening was presenting to me? It didn't matter because I was having a wonderful time with interesting people and it felt good to be there.

Even though this comment completely came out of left field, Gerry knew the person Tom was suggesting and completely agreed that this candidate definitely had possibilities. They went down the list of qualities and characteristics of the future man of the hour for me. He loved the outdoors. He was big into camping and fishing. He was in fantastic shape, nice looking, had a huge heart, was very gentle and, most importantly, he was spiritual.

Well, I had to admit, he sounded pretty good, and then they told me he was a firefighter who had just got out of a really bad relationship. The bad relationship part was not what initially made me pull back from this fantastic idea. No, that was not it at all. It was the fact that this man puts his life on the line every day he goes to work.

I turned to the dynamic duo and said, "Not interested, for a couple of reasons. One, I'm too old for the competition that may be vying for this man's attention every time we are out in public. Two, did you guys just forget the loss that I have just gone through? No, I don't think I could go through that again." They both tried to convince me to at least have a look (like they were trying to sell me a used car and just wanted me to kick the tires).

Then, as if this conversation were not funny enough, Tom just kept adding to the humour of it all. He just remembered that this man happened to be at home right at that very moment and, perhaps, if he gave him a call, maybe Tom could entice him to come over for a piece of pie and a cup of coffee? As he pulled out his cell phone to make the call, I just laughed and decided it was time to go to the kitchen and start the dinner clean up. I did not want to hear how Tom was going to ask "Arnold Schwarzenegger" to get his butt over to Lori's—for what, a shopping spree?

As I was walking toward the kitchen I was thinking to myself that this might just be the best party Lori had ever thrown, should things turn out. Life—Wow! Sometimes it just catches you completely off guard. When you least expect it, that's when some of the most amazing things happen.

Well, sure enough, I was informed about ten minutes later that we were having another person join us for dessert. Okay, I would now have to rank this party as being in the top three for most exciting ever.

To say that I was slightly interested when this "Amazon of a Man" eventually showed up and walked into the room would be a gross understatement. I was laughing hysterically on the inside thinking, *"Is this really happening to me right now? Someone pinch me. Here I am thinking I would come to a party to wish a friend the best of luck and spend some time with other good people, and just have some laughs for the evening. Did I expect to have this creature delivered to me on a silver platter? No, the*

151

most I was expecting was to maybe score a second piece of pie."

All the other guests knew that our new visitor, Ben, was not there just to sample the homemade pie and to wish Tom well. I felt all eyes on us when we happened to be in a room together at the same time. I was awestruck, but also a little apprehensive.

Two thoughts came to my mind as I was secretly observing Ben mingle in the crowd. First, who in their right mind would throw this man out of their life? Unless the two amigos' perception of this individual was not the true picture of this man's character, and he really wasn't all they pumped him up to be.

Second, it didn't look like Ben had laughed in a long time. There was sadness behind those eyes, which he was trying to mask. Because I had become a master of disguises over the last eighteen months when it came to hiding inner most pain, I could easily pick out fellow masqueraders. It's all in the eyes.

As it turned out, Ben and I did not talk to each other that evening. We caught each other's eyes a couple of times and just smiled, but that was pretty much it for contact besides saying hello when introduced to each other. Then we simply said good night when we all headed to our vehicles to end the evening.

Tom and I spoke for awhile outside by my car about my thoughts, what did I think, would I be interested now that I had seen the merchandise. In the end, he gave me Ben's number saying that Ben had said he was definitely not opposed to my calling him, if I felt comfortable doing so. Ben was leaving the next move up to me.

I took the number but definitely had to think about this. Did I want to take a chance? How serious could it really get anyway? Would we have anything in common? Remember what this man does for a living. What is this person looking for? I knew what I needed, so, perhaps I should give him a call to find out what he was looking for instead of getting my information through Tom.

I made the choice to call Ben and ended up having quite a lovely conversation with him. I remember being pleasantly surprised that it was quite easy to talk with him and, before I knew it, we had been on the phone for almost an hour. We made plans to get together for coffee in the next day or two. We did, and ended up becoming fast friends. There was a connection between the two of us and we enjoyed each other's company. That was something I was missing terribly at the time—companionship.

I wrote in my journal that I was thankful for receiving Ben into my life. What a gift I had been given. It was like he was made to order, delivered to my exact specifications. Ask and ye shall receive; the universe will deliver. I had been writing about a partner like the man I was now spending time with on a regular basis. Ben had so many qualities that reminded me of Mel. His love for the outdoors, masculine build, quiet nature, love of music, and culinary expertise. But Ben had something far more alluring and new that I found addictive. It was his spiritual side. Here was a man who went face to face with death every day and could relate to what I had been through. We would talk for hours about serious life issues and experiences. What did they mean? Why are we here? What did we believe in, if anything? Do you believe in God, in a higher power? What's important to us? Then we would recommend books and movies to each other that had spiritual spins.

We ended up reading each other's suggested books or watching our movies together and, in the end, we would marvel at the messages each source gave to us. What a powerful connection. It was such a pleasure to finally speak to, and spend time with, someone who was as interested in this area of life as I was. The more time we spent together, the more my heart got involved. Ben made it easy for me to care for him.

Yet, my inner voice was telling me to run away because he was still wounded and I might end up getting hurt in the end.

Perhaps he was not ready to enter into a new relationship until he dealt with his past demons. At times, I could see the hurt in his eyes and hear the pain in his voice. But one of the things I had come to respect about him was that he was seeking professional help to work through the issues. Ben so wanted to be a better partner the next time around. That takes an incredible amount of courage and is something I admired. I thought, even knowing I could get hurt in the end, that if I could somehow help or assist in his healing process, if we continued very slowly, then perhaps this could work out well for the both of us.

As time went on, I was starting to see what my role was going to be in this relationship. Perhaps the universe put us together because Ben needed a teacher and it was now my turn to play that role. The student was ready and all he needed was a teacher. I came to accept what my role was in the relationship. We only grow ourselves when we can help others grow along side of us. It was my choice to invite this gift into my life at a time when we both needed to learn life lessons from each other—just like the message in Rose's email. A "season" comes into our life because it is now our turn to share, grow and learn. They bring incredible happiness and laughter into our life when we need it the most. The best part of season relationships is that we will teach each other things we never knew before. It's a win/win for both participants.

Never regret something that made you smile. Ben made my heart smile again. I got that spring back in my step. I started to care how I looked and felt, not only physically, but mentally as well. My goal was to concentrate on my body and my mind—eat properly, exercise, read and educate myself on spiritual and other important issues. Continue to search for my own answers in my own time. I have done all of that and am still maintaining that lifestyle today, and I have never felt better.

I have to attribute my recent successes to something I have never experienced until now. I have inner peace and feel very comfortable within my own skin. Over the last two years I have had to dig deep and claw my way back to life, to a new life. What I don't think others realize is that the survivor is not only mourning the loss of his or her spouse, but also the death of their old self.

I have learned so many things about myself that I didn't know. I am not my yesterdays. I don't deal or handle situations the way I did in the past. I feel calmer than ever before. It takes a lot to knock the wind out of my sails. Over the last two years, I got to know who I am and I will say, with no embarrassment or shame, I love the person I have become. If you can really love who you are, I truly believe the best is yet to come, for you and for whoever shares in your life.

I strongly recommend to any survivor or to anyone who has lost a partner, whether it's through a breakup, separation or divorce, that you take time by yourself. This alone time is critical so that you can figure out where you are going, where you want to be, who you are, who you are not, who you want to share your life with, but most importantly—do the ones you have chosen have the right to share in your life?

A second person added into the mix before you have had the chance to find your answers can sometimes steer you in the wrong direction and then your personal search comes to an end. Don't let that happen. Take this time to be mindful and focus on you. Life-changing events are difficult to deal with and, actually, I believe the older we get, the harder these events are to recover from. Let's face it, we are closer to the end than we are to the beginning of life, so we start thinking to ourselves, *"Was that my last chance at love?"*

If and when you find yourself alone, don't view it as something negative. Look at this time as an opportunity to make changes, attain personal growth and search for your answers. Then, before you know it, your season will show up unexpectedly. And when they do, and they will, accept them into your life

155

with open arms. That's what I did, even though I had my reservations throughout this relationship because I was afraid to have my heart damaged again. I'm grateful that I took the risk by inviting Ben into my life, because if you are not taking risks you are not living life at all.

Knowing how much I healed by spending time alone in order to come to terms with my own pain and other issues, I had to give Ben the time that I felt he needed to deal with his old issues before starting a new relationship with me. If we were to make a fresh start with each other, I did not want to have his past invading our future. With everything that I had read, learned and lived over the last couple of years, the choice to give Ben time was not an easy one to make, but one that I knew was the best for both of us.

When we enter into relationships, a big mistake, but one that is done purely out of love, is to feel that we can heal our partners scars. We can to some degree, but, as I have said throughout my story, if someone wants to change the direction of their life, you cannot do it for them. Everyone has to do it for themselves and in their own time.

I have not looked back at this relationship as something that went sour because of something I personally did or didn't do. I know that I brought nothing but happiness and optimism back into Ben's life, and for that I can be proud and not want for anything more. I feel nothing but gratitude for my season. I know that I have grown in my healing process because of that gratitude and would not have traded the relationship for anything. Ben will forever hold a special place in my heart because I learned more things about myself with him. In that process, I helped someone get through a very difficult time in his life, someone who is continuing his own healing process.

I know how truly appreciative Ben was of our season. If this relationship was meant to be, then my season will return to me, and if it doesn't, I am still grateful for the experience. If you allow yourself to be open to others, the learning never ends. That is what makes this life so damn exciting and worth living— each and every time you start over.

Chapter Eleven

Timing is Everything

Time heals all wounds. Why can't time stand still? Where did the time go? We had the time of our lives. Time has gone by way too fast. Time is so precious. We have so little time.

Okay, so you thought it was the weather that everyone talks about. Well, think again. Do you realize how often we talk about time, yet most of us do nothing to capitalize on it, to make the most of it? We are intelligent human beings and we don't have to be smacked up the side of our heads to know that time is in short supply. When we were kids, time went by too slowly and we couldn't wait to be older. As adults, we wish we could have that time back. Some of us want the chance to go back and make things right, or at least have the opportunity to say or do things for someone who is no longer with us. But we know that just is not possible, at least not in this lifetime.

We are walking through our life collecting information from the situations and events that form our history, our yesterdays. We are storing all these experiences in an internal filing cabinet called our memory. That saying, "I only wish that I had known then what I know now," is a redundant statement because you were not ready to know that lesson at that time in your life.

How can we expect, for example, a child to learn a lesson that is intended for an adult? It can't happen, it's just too soon. This is where I believe that if you are not ready or willing to accept the lesson being presented to you, it will pass you by until you are ready for it later on in life. Timing is everything. We are learning our lessons when we are ready to learn them and not any time sooner. We will see the signs when we are at a point in our lives when we are able to accept them. In order to see the signs, you have to believe. None of this can happen until the timing is right. It will not happen until you are ready.

Let's get back to the statement, "Why do I find myself in the same situations over and over again?" Simply put, you are in these same situations because you are constantly focusing your attention on what you don't want, as opposed to putting your energy into the things that you really do want out of life. While on this journey, we have to experience good and bad situations so that we can decide what life is, for ourselves, what we really want from this life. How will you be able to know what you truly want if you have not experienced life and all that it has to offer? If you have led a sheltered life or perhaps have withdrawn from people, events or situations because of fear that you might have gotten hurt or you were afraid of what others would think of you and your decisions, you ended up living your life based on what others expected of you. Well, I'm here to tell you, you should have taken the risks because life is there for the taking and all you have to do is just reach out and grab on. Now, the good thing is that it is never too late to start taking those risks. It's simply a matter of making different choices for yourself.

I am so grateful for all the good things that have happened in my life, but, truth be told, I would have to say that I am even more thankful for all the bad things that have occurred in my past. They have taught me the most valuable of all my lessons because they have given me my boundaries. They have taught me what I definitely do not want in my life and to stay away from it.

Do not pay attention to those situations, or what you don't want, because it's a waste of energy. Case in point: Mel and I didn't acknowledge cancer as part of our daily lives, and I firmly believe that that was what gave us the additional bonus years. We chose to focus on life rather than death, on the positive rather than the negative.

It was the Christmas of 2006 that I received a very special gift. It wasn't the type of gift that was sitting under the tree, wrapped in pretty paper with a bow on it, waiting for me to rip it apart to see the contents. The gift was answers to questions that I had been asking the universe to shed some light on in order for me to be able to move forward. The event that I am about to describe for you will illustrate that the universe is working for us all of the time. There are no coincidences in life. We are in the right place at the right time. Things that happen to us were meant to happen to us, good and bad.

Kiminition: on understanding the incomprehensible events of the past and present:

I want to continue my thoughts regarding eternal beings. Remember, I believe that we all signed those "earthly contracts" that mapped out what, who, when, where and how our earthly existence would unfold. Well, I am still sticking to that belief because it helps me deal with wrapping my mind around situations that are so horrific that if I did not have anything to believe in, I would lose my faith in mankind. I believe those particular eternal beings accepted the horrible terms of their contract because they were selfless in their reasons for coming to Earth in the first place. They agreed to be the unspoken heroes of our time, which meant enduring a portion, or all of their earthly life to great suffering or sacrifice. They did that because either their assault or untimely and cruel death would make the rest of the world stand up, take notice, and work together as a human race to abolish crimes and atrocities committed against our families.

These special beings were the greatest teachers to the world. They taught us and will continue to teach us the ultimate lesson of all. Every life matters, and, that if we stand together, we will all one day experience Heaven on Earth.

When you see the gifts that the universe unfolds right before your eyes, you are in awe and want to share with everyone what you believe to be true. My gift came from my seventeen-year-old niece, Shayla. We were all sitting around shooting the breeze and catching up on each other's lives. My three other sisters (Rose, Pat and Lovey) had flown in to spend part of the holidays with me, my other sister, Debi, and her three daughters. The plan was to spend Christmas Eve and Day with this clan and then, on December 26, Rose, Pat, Lovey and I would jump into my vehicle and drive to the U.S. to spend the remainder of the holidays with my brother and sister-in-law. *(Remember my "new" tradition.)*

Shayla would be graduating from high school that year and we were all asking her what her plans and course options were going to be for university. Shayla is an honour-roll student and subjects such as math and science have always come easily to her, so she is positive that whatever path she chooses, it will have something to do with these subjects.

She was so beautiful when she was telling us about a paper she was writing for one of her classes. She was so passionate about the topic that she said she might want to pursue a career in quantum physics. This paper ended up taking on a life of its own and really made her think about things, about life. She said that she never expected to get so involved and have such a captured interest in what she discovered when doing research for her paper.

Did I just hear her correctly? Did she say quantum physics? I looked at Shayla like she had just grown a second head right before my eyes.

The paper's topic dealt with a "simple" question: "Why are we here?" One of her resource materials was a video called, *What the Bleep Do We Know?* and she touted this movie as one of the most interesting she had ever seen in her life. It had such an effect on her that she was seriously thinking about entering into the wacky, crazy world of quantum physics so that she could perhaps one day tell the world, with scientific proof, why we are here.

This movie asks the viewer some pretty important questions about life. Is this the life that we really want for ourselves? Why do we pick the same partners, jobs and friends over and over again?

I remember thinking to myself at the time, *"My God, how lucky is this child?"* For her to be asking, at such a young age, one of the world's ultimate questions, one that philosophers, scientists and religious leaders have been trying to answer for centuries, completely astounded me. When I was her age, the most monumental question I asked myself was maybe, "Should I get that super-sized?"

I am almost thirty years her senior and I have been asking myself these questions only in the last seven years. More so over the last two years because I was trying to make sense of everything that had happened to me. I would constantly be asking myself, *"What is the meaning of it all anyway?"*

I have never been more proud of Shayla than I was at that very moment. I thought, *"Kiddo, if you can figure that out or at least know why we do the things we do at such a young age, then I cannot wait to see the life that you are going to create for yourself, because you are miles ahead of your elders."* Maybe this generation will really get it right and have it all figured out by the time they are thirty years old. How exciting for them! Can you imagine their possibilities?

My sisters and I eventually got to our brother's home in Minneapolis and it was just wonderful being there with Fred and Denise. This new tradition of being someplace other than my home during the holidays and our wedding anniversary has been a godsend for me. True to form, we all pretty much did the same thing that Christmas as we had the previous year, which was nothing—and that's the way we like it.

I'll try to give you a visual of a typical day for our family during this time. We all get up between eight and ten a.m. Have a nice healthy breakfast and go through a number of pots of freshly brewed java. We will do a quick clean up and then will play a number of card and/or dice games *(for money)* while listening to wonderful music *(of course, still in our pajamas)* and usually laughing our heads off, because we always seem to find humour in almost everything or every topic that is mentioned when sitting around with each other.

Lunch will then be served and, because some of us are feeling a little guilty about not doing a thing all day, maybe someone will go and have a shower to be a little more respectable, while the others throw the dishes into the dishwasher. We will reconvene and go back to playing more games, listening to music, laughing and snacking. Before we know it, it's supper time and we are eating again *(most of us are still in our pajamas)*.

We will do more dishes and then retire to the basement to watch at least two, and sometimes three movies on the big screen TV. By three or four in the morning we are saying good night/morning to one another *(It works out so well that most of us are still in our pajamas because we can just flop into our beds)*. Then the next morning we follow the same routine, and love every single minute of it.

Holidays are a time to unwind and break from our everyday busy schedules and timetables. We are not driven or controlled by alarm clocks. There are no meetings or customers to visit with. There are no deadlines to meet. There is no one to try to make a good impression on. It is a time to sit back, relax, and enjoy being with the people you love. We have an absolute blast doing nothing and the best presents that we offer each other during the holidays are the gifts of laughter and love.

It was either the first or second night that Fred mentioned he had a movie he thought we would really like to see. He was quite impressed with it and was excited for us to see it and get our take on it. The name of the movie was, *What the Bleep Do We Know?*

Do you believe it? I was totally shocked. Fred had no idea that only two days prior to this moment his niece had been saying the exact same thing to her aunties. A coincidence? I don't think so.

Well, of course, we all had to see this video because this was the second glowing review from our own family's Siskel and Ebert. I could not believe that we were going to be holding off watching an academy award winning DVD that was most likely sitting in the stack of movies in order to watch a movie on quantum physics. *(Yes! How exciting! Hold on, before we start that movie let me go find my pocket protector and make sure my Bunsen burner is turned off! What a bunch of dweebs.)*

We put the movie in and I was instantly engrossed. This movie hit so close to home for me because it was a compilation of almost everything I had been reading or watching over the last two years or so. Things like, Why are we here? What is our purpose? What and who is God? Spirituality versus religion and religion versus science. How powerful are our thoughts? *(A fantastic experiment with water was shown to illustrate the power of thoughts in this movie; let's just say it blew my mind.)* What is reality? Is reality what the brain processes or what the eyes see? Do we create our own reality? Are we exploring new possibilities when we start asking ourselves hard questions? Are we addicted to our emotions? Do we love ourselves? Have we taken a good, hard look at who we are?

There were so many times during that movie I wanted to stand up and say, "Yeah, *exactly that happened to me. Or, oh my God, I never thought that's the reason why that happens or better yet, that's the reason why they act like that.*"

Then there were times I cried. I know, I can't believe I am saying it either. I actually cried watching a movie about quantum physics. I could now totally relate to Shayla's excitement and passion about considering this area of science as a possible career choice.

Damn it, I think I want to enroll in university and get into the world of this amazing, complex study of physics to understand and then announce to everyone, *"The search is over. I, Kim Malchuk, have found and can back up with scientific evidence why we are here. It is not a mistake and I will tell you everything you want to know, just step into my lab."* Okay, so do you think I liked the movie?

I was thrilled to have finally seen and heard something of a scientific nature that proved to me that I wasn't alone in my thinking. Maybe I was on the right track about how our choices pave the road of our lives, how people can be addicted to emotions, about HP not being so judgmental, and the limitations we put on ourselves by not letting go of the past.

Others were speaking my language and asking the same questions I desperately wanted answers to as well. I don't want to come off as though I know it all because that could not be further from the truth. I have only begun to scratch the surface of so many topics and areas of life about which I still need to know why, how, where, when and who. But there are things I do know and I think this is probably the biggest reason I sat down to write this book. When I finally decided to sit down and put my lessons learned down on paper in hopes of helping others, the words just simply flowed onto the paper.

This book is definitely a tribute to my husband and the love that we shared; there is no doubt about that. But it is about so much more, and not just for survivors but for anyone who has ever lost a partner. This is also for anyone who is starting to question themselves about where they are on their life's journey. It's for the people who continually find themselves in the same situations and cannot see things ever changing. It's for the people who say they are stuck in a rut and can't seem to get out of it. It's for the person who is continuing to blame others for their unhappiness or for their empty life. It's for the person who is always falling victim to life's tests that are constantly being thrown at them.

Timing is Everything

I wrote this book because I have lived in some of these states at one time or another in my life, but not anymore. It really is not that difficult to turn things around if you really and truly want to discover the gifts that this life has to offer all of us. All you have to do is believe in yourself.

After watching the video, I literally jumped off the couch and announced to my family at that very moment that I needed to do something to change the world. Okay, I know I was a little dramatic, but you get the point, right?

It was right around this time that I was writing in my journals that I needed to start thinking about how I plan to help people. I remember writing that I thought some of the things I was writing could possibly help other survivors, people who find themselves alone in this world when they don't want to be, or people who were just struggling with life in general. I felt that I had something to share and to say. My life had made a complete 180-degree turn in a matter of two years and I was truly excited to live life again. I wondered then, if someone read my story, could I actually make them excited about their life as well?

I walked away from watching that movie excited about the new possibilities and honestly believed that the best was yet to come for me. I didn't know how it was going to unfold but that wasn't for me to worry about. I just knew that there was something much bigger waiting for me to discover and to tap into. There was a reason why I saw this movie. It was telling me to explore new possibilities, not to limit myself. If you really put your mind to it, anything is possible.

If someone had told me two years ago that I would be saying that I have not yet lived the best years of my life, I would have laughed in their face and said they were out of their mind. The best years of my life were the years I shared with Mel. There is no denying that. But now I will refer back to Rose's email again about the people who come into our lives for a "lifetime".

The years, lessons, truths and experiences that I shared with Mel gave me the foundation to carry on and build even stronger and more meaningful relationships for the remainder of my life. The bar has been set and boundaries are in place. I know that I will never settle for anything less than what I shared with Mel. My goal is to have the same or better and, should it happen that I never find that again, I am completely and honestly okay with that possibility. I know how fortunate I was to have experienced that kind of love, even once in my lifetime. To get it twice, well, that would be a miracle, but I am a firm believer that miracles do happen to people who really want them to happen.

Before Mel came into my life, I asked myself the question, "What is my purpose in life?" I believe we have many purposes, not just one. Once we find a purpose and fulfill it, it's time for the next because that is how we grow as individuals. I felt that I was at my best when I was with Mel. I was at my highest potential and could do anything I put my mind to. I had evolved into the woman I knew was there but was waiting for the right time to emerge, for that perfect situation.

When I said I wanted to challenge myself all those years ago, the universe answered my calling. Remember what I said earlier about being careful what you wish for because the universe will always deliver? It was a good thing that I was serious about what I was asking for. There were times that Mel tried to push me away and not have me be a part of his life because of his situation and because of the pain our love would cost me in the end, but I insisted that I needed to be by his side. I didn't know why I was chosen or why he showed up exactly at the time in my life that he did, but I told him he would just have to trust me. He did, and we ended up having the most incredible ride of our lives.

I know that we shocked each other and were consistently amazed that our union was so solid from the day we decided to go forward as a couple, considering the odds we faced. I was up for the challenge the universe was presenting to me because that was what I truly wanted and asked for. Mel was my purpose, and learning to live life to the fullest with cancer hovering over our heads was the test of all tests. I passed that test with flying colours and have no regrets for inviting Mel into my life. To this day, that is by far the best choice I ever made because it afforded me the opportunity to learn so much about the person inside of me.

What is next on the agenda for my life? How can I go forward and make a difference? What is my new purpose? With all the reading, and then seeing that movie, it was almost like the universe was screaming at me to do something. But what is it?

I remember getting a call from my sister Rose, who had to tell me about something she had heard from a very good friend of hers who is very spiritual. She told me about a movie called *The Secret* and how it's the latest buzz that has everyone talking. It is basically a step-by-step guide about how to achieve what you want out of life. I said that I would check it out. Timing is everything, as I've said before. If we were not where we are today, we would not be able to see and hear the messages that are out there waiting for each of us to discover.

I am not pushing anyone to read or watch anything in particular. I am not telling you what you should believe in or not believe in. I am also not favouring spirituality over religious practices. I am just sharing my personal experiences, which have led to huge and positive changes in my life.

The Secret reconfirmed so many of the messages and facts that I have read over the past few years. Did I learn anything earth shattering from watching it? No. Do I watch it over and over again? You're darn tootin' I do! It is great to hear and have a constant reminder from scientists, theologians, successful entrepreneurs and authors that we are creating our own future, our own destiny every day. We are getting exactly what we want and, yes, that includes all the crap. How are we doing that? By the choices we make.

That is what my main message has been throughout this book. Choices guide us to our final place at the end of every day. If you are not happy with where you are sitting at the end of that day, who is responsible for that? Who is to be held accountable for where you are in your life today? The answer is obvious. The common denominator in your life is YOU!

What do you really want out of life and are you absolutely clear about that? If you are, you are miles ahead of millions of people. If you are clear and know exactly what you want out of life, are you getting it? If you are—FANTASTIC! If not, why not?

If you know what you want, but are not getting it, here's *The Secret* in a nutshell. You must be focusing on what you don't want and that is what the universe is giving back to you. The universe cannot distinguish between good and bad; it just knows to give you more of the same. You need to focus on what you want and not worry about how it is going to happen. Trust me. I have given you examples of that throughout this book.

I wanted to start my life over again. I did it. I wanted a new career. I got it. I wanted Mel in my life. I got him. I wanted time with Mel. I got it. I wanted to travel. I did. I wanted a summer home. I got it. I wanted to be able to love my home again. I got it. I wanted to be able to love again. I got it. I wanted to write and publish this book to help people. I DID IT!

This is a really good place to recount what people have said to me often. Considering the loss that I have gone through, the people close to me are amazed at how I have turned my life around. They say things like, *"You are very lucky, Kim"* or *"I just can't believe your good fortune, someone must be looking out for you."*

Luck, or fate, have nothing to do with where I am today. I have consciously chosen to live a positive life and be so grateful for everything and everyone that has come into my life. Once I made those choices and continually thanked the universe for everything in my life *(on a daily basis)*, a lot of special things started to occur in my life. Some of my very close friends and family can attest to this change of events. It's absolutely amazing, and this is what I want to share with you, because you can have this too. You just have to choose differently, but there is a catch to all of this good fortune.

In order for the things that you really want to manifest in your life, you have to truly believe that you deserve them. Do you deserve a better life? Of course you do. We all do, because that is our right. All you have to do is start visualizing and acting like you already have it. You have to focus on what you want and not pay any more attention to the things you do not want in your life. You need to truly believe that you deserve what you want out of life, because if you don't honestly feel it, it's not going to happen.

You have to change your thoughts because it is our thoughts that attract all things into our lives. If your thoughts are happy and positive, you will attract more of that—and then, of course, you know the flip side of that coin. We have all heard or know of someone who is constantly complaining about their health and have convinced themselves that they are sick, and guess what? They end up getting sick. Same with friends and family who are constantly looking at the glass half empty, or who continue to play the role of the victim.

Energy seeks its own level. Like attracts like. This is not a hard concept to follow or to understand. This is the way life works. Thoughts and feelings are energy and energy is life. There is a beautiful quote by the Buddha (also mentioned in *The Secret*) that says in a much more powerful way what I am trying to say here: *"All that we are is the result of what we have thought."*

Chapter Twelve

The Choice is Up to You

You may be, at this very moment, going through your own grieving process, whether it is due to death, separation, break up or divorce. These life-changing events share common emotions, perhaps on a different scale, but nonetheless, there are commonalities. So what are they?

The survivor, the one left behind, the one who didn't want what happened to happen, has to learn to live life on his or her own again. They are flying solo and this can be a very scary prospect. Depending on your age, some of these events can be very difficult to get through. But I am here to tell you that you will get through it in your own time and will definitely be a stronger person for it. Well, if not stronger, definitely different, but because I don't know you personally, I have faith and am positive that this event will only make you a better person.

If I were a betting person and could have placed a sure bet on my state of mind, body, outlook and health two years ago, I would have been "all in" and said that I would never get over the loss of my husband. I would definitely never let love into my life again because it was just too painful in the end. Good thing I didn't do that because I would be sitting here naked right now and hand writing all my thoughts out to you on paper as opposed to my computer because I would have lost everything on that bet. I was so sure that I would never get over the loss. The solitude, loneliness, despair, tears and emptiness made me truly understand where someone has to be when they are considering taking their own life. It is the darkest place I have ever been to and never want to return. It is equivalent to being buried alive.

I tried to share with you the depth of our love so that you would understand what our life was like. I hope that I did that and conveyed to you that love like ours really does exist out there. I was very skeptical, believing that the love we have seen depicted by Hollywood was only the great imagination of writers and never to really be experienced in life. Boy was I wrong, and so pleasantly surprised when it came my way. I think that was when I really started to let my guard down and stop being pessimistic about other things in life. If I was wrong about love, then maybe I was also wrong about a lot of other things too.

Admitting your mistakes, or that you were wrong, is one of the biggest steps you can make in turning your life around. In doing that you are taking responsibility for the outcomes of your choices, all of your choices. I believe it takes a very courageous person to admit their errors or bad choices, because they are opening themselves up to external exposure and possible ridicule. Stop looking at it that way. The payoff is that the burden you carry around with you is lighter.

Just think about how you feel when you say you are sorry and the other person accepts your apology. You feel great. You feel lighter. When you are lighter, you are happier. When you are happier, you are more accepting and positive. When you are positive, you attract positive things.

Life has a ripple effect and the universe picks up on the energy we emit. It is a fact that most men have a very difficult time saying they are sorry, even when they are 100 percent at fault. Most men cannot muster the strength to look the other person in the eye and tell them how truly sorry they are. Why? Because that would be admitting they made a mistake. Men— stop it! This is why women are outliving you. Women do not have a hard time saying they are sorry. Sometimes I think we say it too much: *"Sorry to bother you, sorry I bumped into you, sorry I forgot to call you, blah, blah, blah."*

The point is that when you take responsibility for your choices, good and bad, and admit you made a mistake, the minute you say it, it's done and it's over. It's in the past and you are not your past. To move forward, you need to lighten the load. If you do not stop concentrating on your past, how will you ever be able to make room for your future?

As it is with admitting your mistakes, an easy way to lighten that same load is to forgive yourself. Remember, it is a sign of strength to be able to forgive, not a sign of weakness. The more you practice forgiving yourself, the easier you will find it to forgive others. We are all trying to find our way in this life and for those of us who are continually making mistakes along that road, good for us! We are the brave ones. We should be proud of our mistakes because it is from those situations that we learn the most. If you have done something wrong or bad along this journey, forgive yourself and don't do it again.

The point is to stop beating yourself up for past mistakes. You are learning and in order to learn you have to make mistakes. Why do you think pencils have a built-in eraser? Life expects you to make mistakes, just like that pencil does. What you do to your today does not have to make your tomorrow!

Positive thoughts are the critical element for everything. I tried to give you as many real-life situations that happened to me when I lived in a positive state as opposed to a negative one. I cannot believe my good fortune of late, but then I can because I look at what I am sending out to the universe and I have nothing but positive thoughts inside me. So why shouldn't all these amazing things happen to me? I honestly cannot remember the last time I got angry. My days are filled with such gratitude that I constantly catch myself giggling to myself. I literally cannot wait to get up every morning to see what wonderful and exciting thing is going to happen to me, and that is the truth.

I am going to give you three separate events that have happened to me recently that will substantiate the power of positive thinking. Just like I had wished someone were in the car with me that night driving home when I saw the formation of clouds smiling down on me *(I mean besides my cat)* my eternal sister, Hayley, was with me when all of these recent great things happened. Hayley is totally convinced that I am the "chosen one". Of course, we laugh about that and I simply tell her it's because I am creating my own reality.

The first event was that I injured myself at one of our baseball games this summer. I had torn my ligaments in my left ankle and the doctor told me that it looked like I would be out for the remainder of the season. I said no to that diagnosis, that I would only be off for three to four weeks. The doctor just shook his head and said, "well, we will just see about that." I was off for four weeks and both my doctor and physiotherapist could not believe how fast I healed and said that it was a miracle considering how bad my X-rays were. *(Hmmm ... miracle or positive attitude?)*

The second event happened when Hayley and I went shopping for outfits for a friend's upcoming wedding. We were having a blast in this one store when the assistant manager came up to me, gave me her business card and a job application and asked me if I would think about working in her store a couple of nights a week. No interview necessary. Hayley and I couldn't believe that I was being offered a job completely out of the blue, especially when I didn't need one. I called the assistant manager two weeks later and guess what? I am working two nights a week at this lovely woman's clothing store and getting a fantastic employee discount to boot. *(Hmmm … miracle or positive attitude?)*

Now for the third one. I saved the best for last because this is a great example of how powerful our thoughts can be. One night after our baseball game, our team went out for pizza to the restaurant that sponsors our team. Long story short, a man attempted to give me his number in the parking lot when I was on my way to my vehicle. I completely misread the situation and totally disregarded him and thought that it was a joke. *(I have been out of practice for a while, what can I say.)*

After I realized that I had just made a huge mistake, I wanted to flag his vehicle down to explain my ignorance. That didn't happen but it bothered me all day and for many days after that. I talked to Hayley about it, saying that I wasn't sure why this encounter bothered me, but I was so sorry for my actions and that I just could not stop thinking about my treatment of this stranger.

Okay, so here comes the good part. For a few days I kept saying to myself that I would really like the opportunity to apologize for my conduct to this man. That's it. I just kept thinking that to myself. Anyway, seven days later at a completely different establishment, in a completely different area of the city, I got my opportunity because this same stranger walked in and sat down almost right in front of me. Hayley could not believe it. All I said was that if she didn't believe me now about how powerful thoughts can be, I wasn't sure what I would have to do next to convince her that positive thinking will really make things happen.

We both got a little emotional because, quite frankly, that was pretty significant for this stranger to show up just because I truly and honestly wanted it to happen. It took a little time for me to muster up the courage to walk up to him to apologize for my previous actions, but I did and both he and I laughed about it afterwards. No hard feelings. There is a line in *The Secret* that goes something like this, "When you are feeling good all the time and living in the magic, start visualizing your wants and things will start to materialize." They're not kidding! WOW! I am still amazed at that one.

It has now been over two years that I have been alone and I am so grateful for the time I've had, and continue to have, because I have learned so much about myself that I never knew before. Embrace your alone time. If you can't stand being with yourself, what does that say to others about you? Take this time as a time of discovery. It's a chance to do what you want on your own terms, nobody telling you what to do, where to be, when to call, what to buy, who to see, etc. It is your own downtime so play, learn, read, test, visit, pamper, exercise, educate, travel, laugh, cry, and, explore during this time. I can guarantee you will find out things about yourself that you had no idea you were capable of or interested in. Introduce yourself to you. Learn about the person within and I bet *(because I am a betting person)* that you will love the person you will meet. If you can truly love yourself, then you are ready to go out and find your "Mel" and ask them if they would like to join in on the party of your life. The person who you will be inviting in will see that you are glowing and loving life, and, because of that, you will be attracting the same type of person.

It is a fact that when a person has inner peace, all other good things will come naturally. It's the Law of Attraction. You attract what you are putting out there every single day.

I can honestly say that I believe the day I jumped out of that airplane and landed so beautifully on the ground was the day I started to be sincerely thankful for everything in my life. I was thankful to be alive. I was grateful for the enormous number of lessons I learned over the past six years with Mel and since then. I am thankful for my friends and family, who have continued to be with me during this time. I am thankful for my overall health. I am thankful to my reasons and my seasons for what they have brought into my life. I am grateful to it all. I love where I am sitting now. I have to be grateful to everything because it was all part of the plan to get me to this spot. I really believe that if you are honestly grateful for the positive things in your life, you will attract more of the same.

I was at my trailer one weekend and threw in one of my all-time favourite movies. It's a movie that just makes me feel good and one that I can watch over and over again because of the beautiful and simple messages it offers. The movie is *Forrest Gump*. When I was watching it, I was almost finished writing this book and I thought perhaps this would be a good way to end my story because it ties in quite nicely with everything in this chapter.

For those of you unfamiliar with the movie, I will give you the Reader's Digest version. It starts with a shot of a single white feather floating in the sky and eventually landing on Forrest's shoe at a bus stop, where he is telling complete strangers his remarkable life story. Forrest is going to visit the love of his life, Jenny. *Forrest Gump* is about a simple-minded man who achieved extraordinary things in life. It's the story of a man who loved everyone, and, was loved by all who came into his life. I think the main message in this movie is that living a simple and easy life can bring you many riches.

As humans, we complicate things far too often. If it's harder it must be better, because if it's easy it can't be good. Where did we go so wrong with this kind of thinking? The messages in the books and movies I have read or seen over the last two years are all basically the same things being repeated time and time again. This information is not rocket science. It is simply bringing us back to the basics and reminding us that happy thoughts, positive thinking, a simple and uncomplicated life, forgiveness and love will bring you what you want in life and much, much more.

I am going to leave you with one more little miracle that happened that same evening. Just another example of what can happen when your heart is filled with peace and blissfulness.

After I watched this movie, I was packing up the trailer and starting to take things to my vehicle for the ride home. I was smiling and feeling so at peace with having watched this touching movie again. A thousand different thoughts were running through my head and I was grateful that I chose to watch the movie to end off another great weekend before heading back to the city. It gave me a sense of calmness. I started to think that I was definitely going to throw something about Forrest into my book. Even though the story is fictional, the message is there for those who can pick up on it. A simple life can make dreams come true.

On my second trip back to my vehicle, I was thinking about how I would fit Forrest into my book or was it just a silly idea that I should forget? As I was walking back to my vehicle, I got my answer in the most remarkable and beautiful way. I saw something laying on the ground right beside my car. Was it there before? I don't think so because I am sure that I would have noticed it. As I approached this white object, I thought that I maybe had dropped a piece of paper or Kleenex on my first trip out to the car. But as I bent down to have a closer look to see what the object was, I was pleasantly surprised to see that it was neither a piece of paper or tissue. It was a single white feather that must have floated down from the sky and landed right by my vehicle. I stood there with tears in my eyes, looking up towards the sky, completely amazed and thought to myself, *"Isn't life grand?"*

Thank You...

...for inviting me into your life so I could share my story with you. Wherever you are in your journey, there is a reason you chose to read this book at this time in your life. Was it to simply occupy your mind so that you could escape reality for a few hours? Was it because you are questioning your own path in life? Was it because you are wondering about the choices you have made along the way? It doesn't really matter, because we found each other and that is all that is important.

I hope my story entertained you, made you laugh, think, question and cry, but most importantly, my biggest hope is that it made you think about the possibilities for yourself. Do you want to change the direction of your life? The choice is yours. It always has been and will be. That will never change. Will you?

Attention: Book Club Members

If you are an active book club member
or are interested in starting your own book club
visit my website

www.TastingRain.com

to learn more details about Book Club Packages

Enjoy the Rain!

You matter to me!

Tasting Rain was written with one goal in mind —
to HELP others.
I wrote the book for you and I truly hope that our
meeting does not end here.
It is important to me, as the writer of
this story, to know if
Tasting Rain made an impact on you.

I invite you to share your thoughts with me by
sending an email to kim@tastingrain.com or
posting a comment on my BLOG at
www.TastingRain.com.

The length of your message does not matter. What
does matter is that you have a voice and I thank you in
advance for sharing that with me, so until then...

Enjoy the Rain!